Values
for Thinking

ROBERT FISHER

Nash Pollock
Publishing

Acknowledgements

I am grateful to the many people who have helped in my research into teaching values in primary schools, in particular to Dishi Attwood, Sarah Burke, Paul Cleghorn, Claire Hughes, Sara Liptai, Lizann O'Conor, Marziyah Panju, Bernadette Sheridan, Vicky Taylor, Stella Ware, Robert Watts and Jo Young who have helped me to trial the use of the materials in the classroom. I also wish to thank Roger Sutcliffe and others in SAPERE, the organisation for promoting Philosophy for Children, who have helped to pioneer the use of philosophical discussion for teaching thinking, citizenship and moral values in UK schools.

I wish to thank the following for generous permission to use copyright material in this book: Lenono Music for the lyrics of 'Imagine' by John Lennon; Fitzwilliam Museum Cambridge for permission to reproduce 'I want! I want!' by William Blake; P.J. Walsh for 'The Bully Asleep' by the late John Herbert Walsh from *Poets in Hand* (Puffin, 1985); Bernard Young for the poem 'Best Friends' by permission of the author; the Metropolitan Police for use of a recruitment photo; and Tom Fisher for the drawing accompanying 'Why?'

© 2001 Robert Fisher

First published in 2001 by
Nash Pollock Publishing
32 Warwick Street
Oxford OX4 1SX

9 8 7 6 5 4 3 2 1

Orders to:
York Publishing Services
64 Hallfield Road
Layerthorpe
York YO31 7ZQ

A catalogue record of this book is available from the British Library.

ISBN 1 898255 37 7

Design, typesetting and production management by
Black Dog Design, Buckingham

Printed in Great Britain by Bath Press Limited, Bath

Contents

Introduction

What are values?

People are always doing wrong things. To change what they do you have to change the way they think.   Ray, aged 12

Create a society where people matter more than things.
                                            Archbishop Desmond Tutu

When her teacher asked, 'What are the most important things in your life?' Karen, aged 6, answered, 'What is most important to me is me.' As Karen suggests, our values are closely connected to who we are and how we think of ourselves. Our sense of values begins with beliefs about oneself and what is important in one's life. If children are to develop a sense of self-identity and self-awareness we must help them to know who they are, and what they think, believe and feel. Values are rooted in our experience of and response to the world. Children need help in making sense of their experience and in finding answers to the question: 'What does it mean for me?'

What are values?

A suggested definition of 'values' is:

Fundamental beliefs or principles which determine our attitude to, and guide our judgement of, behaviour and the worth of things, including what is right or wrong, good or bad, important or unimportant.

Values are fundamental expressions of what we think and believe. They reflect our personal concerns and preferences (eg 'I prefer x to y'), but values are also inter-personal. They help to frame our relationships with others. As children mature they need to develop moral values that help them to make sense of increasingly complex relationships with other people. They need to make judgements relating to others, about what to think and how to behave (eg 'It would be kind to Sally to …'). They need to become aware of the thoughts and feelings of others, to think about their experience of others and find answers to the question 'What does it mean for others?'

Values are also social and relate to people living in communities and in society (eg 'It should be a rule that…'). We need to help them think about the values that relate to living together in society. Values are not just preferences or moral judgements, they are about a way of life that is internally lived yet socially constituted. There are rights and duties for all who live in a community or society. In a democracy all have a contribution to make to the discussion of rights and duties, and how society should function. As Manesh, aged 8, said: 'A democracy means we all decide together.' Social values reflect our understanding as citizens, and help to find answers to questions such as 'What does it mean for the community (or society)?'

Values for Thinking is about enquiring into these three key aspects of values:

- *Personal values* – values in relation to self
- *Moral values* – values in relation to others
- *Social values* – values in relation to a community or society

There are many other values in which education is grounded, such as spiritual, cultural, environmental, aesthetic and political values. These also comprise the subject matter of this book. Education is about knowledge and curriculum content but it is also about the development of values. Knowledge deals with 'what is' whereas values deals with 'what is good or bad' and 'what ought to be'. Value judgements are involved in every aspect of the curriculum. As Maria, aged 11, observed: 'What we are talking about is not just lessons, but what is important in our lives.'

One of the challenges children face today is how to make sense of the messages they receive through the media, through school and home and through contact with others, about what they should think of themselves and of others, about how to behave, and about problems in the community. Children face a bewildering range of conflicting messages about the choices that face them, and it is no wonder that many are confused about what they think and what they should do. Lucy, aged 9, summed the problem up as follows: 'It's because there are so many choices that we don't know what to think.'

What is Values Education?

Values education covers a range of curriculum experience including:

- personal, social and health education (PSHE)
- citizenship education
- school assembly
- spiritual and religious education
- cultural education
- environmental education
- pastoral care
- school ethos
- community involvement

Children need help to meet these challenges by developing a set of inter-related values including personal, moral and social values.

Personal values reflect what one thinks is important, good or right in life. A child's awareness of their personal values, and what they think and feel to be important is part of what could be called their personal (or metacognitive) intelligence.[1] Personal intelligence means knowing oneself, and being able to take responsibility for what one thinks and does in life. When Sean, aged 8, was asked to reflect on what he had learnt from a Values for Thinking discussion, he replied: 'It made me think about what I think.' Part of the purpose of this book is to help children become more mindful about what they think and do – and so develop their personal intelligence, including self-awareness and self-esteem.

Personal values related to the self include:

* understanding of oneself, our own character, strengths and weaknesses
* developing self control, self respect and self discipline
* showing perseverance in making the most of our talents and abilities
* growing self confidence to stand up for what is right
* taking responsibility for the way we lead our lives

A key aim of this book, and of personal, social and health education (PSHE) is to encourage the self-awareness, self-esteem and self confidence of children as thinkers and learners, and to help them value themselves as unique human beings capable of spiritual, moral, intellectual and physical self development.

What is personal, social and health education?

Children and young people need the self-awareness, positive self-esteem and confidence to:

* stay as healthy as possible
* keep themselves and others safe
* have worthwhile and fulfilling relationships
* respect the differences between people
* develop independence and responsibility
* play an active role as members of a democratic society
* make the most of their own and others' abilities

Source: QCA (2000)

Moral values are beliefs about what is right or wrong, good or bad. These beliefs generate principles and influence the ways we behave. Some moral values have personal consequences, and can affect the way you behave. As Omar, aged 10, said: 'If you think that telling lies is wrong you don't tell so many lies.' The themes in this book aim to help children reflect on moral issues and to consider what behaviour would bring the best results for themselves and others – and thus develop their moral awareness and intelligence.

Moral values concern our relationships with others and these are also fundamental to a fulfilled and happy life. Values related to others and our relationships with them include:

- respect for others, irrespective of race, gender, social group or ability
- care for others and the exercise of courtesy towards them
- loyalty, trust and friendship
- co-operation with others and the ability to share
- patience, tolerance and the ability to resolve conflicts peacefully

Children need to learn to value others for themselves, not just for what they have or can do for us, and to see that relationships based on fairness and care are fundamental for ourselves and the community.

Social values are beliefs which generate principles to which we think the behaviour of members of society should conform. These beliefs are social if they are about the principles of right and wrong in society. Social values relate moral and personal beliefs to the wider community. Ravinder, aged 8, expressed a social value when he defined the key principle of democratic discussion, in the classroom and in society, as: 'Everyone should have the chance to speak and say what they think.'

Social values are concerned with the good of society, the environment and global community. Social values inform a vision of, and commitment to, the sort of world we want to live in. Values related to society and the world beyond might include commitments to:

- truth, justice, freedom, equality and human rights
- respect for justice and the rule of law
- recognition of the importance of love and commitment
- responsibility as active citizens within a democracy
- concern for maintaining a sustainable environment for the future

This book aims to encourage children to think about social values, to become aware of and involved in the life and concerns of their community and society – and so develop both their social intelligence and their capacity to be active and effective future citizens.

> ### *What is citizenship education?*
>
> Education for citizenship includes three inter-related strands:
>
> - *Social and moral responsibility*. Learning self-confidence and socially and morally responsible behaviour towards those in authority and towards each other.
> - *Community involvement*. Learning how to become helpfully involved in the life and concerns of their neighbourhood and communities.
> - *Political literacy*. Learning about the institutions, issues, problems and practices of our democracy and how citizens can make themselves effective in public life, locally, regionally and nationally through skills and values as well as knowledge.
>
> Source: QCA (2000)

Children need opportunities to think about and explore personal, moral and social values, all of which help to build the qualities and skills that develop emotional intelligence. According to Daniel Golman there are 'two different kinds of intelligence, rational and emotional. How we do in life is determined by both – it is not just IQ but emotional intelligence that matters. Indeed, intellect cannot work at its best without emotional intelligence.' Children need to explore their own emotions and the emotions of others (see Appendix 1 and Theme 7, p 57). They need to learn how to discuss and resolve the emotional conflicts, problems and challenges of living with others. They need to learn how to effectively express their views to others, to be open to the views of others, and to learn how they can contribute to making a difference for the better. As Manesh, aged 9, put it: 'We are learning, so we can make a better people and a better world.'

In today's world children are bombarded with messages telling them what they should think and believe. They are surrounded with more information than they will ever need. How to make sense of it all is a problem we all face. As Sarah, aged 7, complained, having found a bewildering array of information available to her on the internet: 'How do I know what I need when there's so much stuff?' Children like Sarah face the challenge of trying to find out not only what is important but what is true. They are also exposed to negative and exploitative messages, focused on their most self-centred needs. They live in a society that perpetuates some potentially damaging myths. One myth is that happiness derives from having a lot of money, a second is that it is achieved by buying the latest consumer goods. A third myth is that happiness is to be found in the world of things outside them, rather than what is in themselves and in their relationships others. As Jason, aged 9, said: 'If you haven't got the things others have got it makes you unhappy.' When his teacher, and others in the class, probed Jason's idea further the children came to a different view, namely that the most important 'things' in life were not the things you owned but the people you loved and the people who loved you.

If education is more than just gaining knowledge, but is also about developing personal values – learning to value oneself and others, and to be an active and responsible citizen in a democracy – the question remains, how should values be taught? We cannot wait in the hope that society will change so that children are not faced with difficult decisions and moral dilemmas, or rely on the hope that children will make the right choices if left to themselves. We must help the children to see that there are real choices to be made about what to think and do, and that they have the power to make those choices and to make a difference in the world. As Joanna, aged 7, summed up her learning in a Values for Thinking lesson as: 'We are learning how to make choices for ourselves.'

In many countries there is a growing concern about the problem of teaching moral values. Changes in society, including uncertain patterns of work, increased social mobility, the fragmentation of family life, conflicting values and life styles, and threats to the political and social order, are challenges which face all modern societies. How should schools respond to conflicting beliefs and values in society? What moral values should we teach and how should we teach them?

What values should we teach?

'We should think what we do, and do what we think, so long as it's right.'
Max, aged 8

The simple answer might be that we need to teach children what is 'right' and 'wrong'. In this view teaching consists in upholding certain fundamental or core values, such as telling the truth, caring for others and following the right rules. But no matter how 'right' we think our values may be, if we simply tell children what to believe they may not accept or internalise them as their own beliefs and values. As Claire, aged 9, said: 'Other people can tell you what to think, but unless you believe it you won't tell yourself.'

If there are reasons for saying that certain beliefs or actions are right or wrong then children need to know what those reasons are. They need to learn that all moral acts have reasons, and they need the skills that will help them to deal with the moral conflicts that they will face in an uncertain world. As 8-year old Paul put it: 'The trouble is people are telling you to do different things, and sometimes your mind tells you to do different things too!'

Children are characterised by conflicting tendencies – to be generous and to be selfish, to be competitive and to be co-operative, to love and hate and so on. Living with others means sometimes coming into conflict with their needs and wishes. In trying to teach children to be thoughtful and reasonable persons, with the capacity for resolving conflicts in themselves and in society, we must see that their experience of life in school and home is as thoughtful and reasonable as possible. Moral education, as opposed to moral indoctrination, cannot be conducted without treating children as rational beings capable of thinking and reasoning about conduct. One way to achieve this is to create a 'community of enquiry' in the classroom, which provides the opportunity for children to discuss values in a systematic, sustained and serious way (see below). But what are the values that should be discussed and developed in a community such as a school or home? What values reflect children's personal, moral and social concerns? What values will motivate them to make a difference for the better for themselves and the community?

Values guide human behaviour. They are beliefs that can be expressed in action. The problem is that there is no one list of definitive values that all would agree on. There are however values which derive from the fact we can only survive by living in supportive social groups. As individuals we may be impelled by selfish needs, but if we are to live in groups we need to have beliefs and organising ideas that harmonise our egocentric needs with the needs and wants of others. Certain values that make social living possible are common to all human cultures. Other values are bound by the context of a particular culture or religion.

In recent years there has been much debate about whether there are any shared, common or core values which should underpin education in a pluralist society. Are there any core values that can be universally accepted? Certain values such as truth-telling and the rule of law are widely shared for without them it would be impossible for society to function. The following values, expressed as what is 'right' or 'wrong', seem to be common to most if not all social, cultural and religious groups:

'Right'	*'Wrong'*
telling the truth	dishonesty
keeping promises	cheating
respecting the rights of others	bullying
respecting the property of others	theft
caring for others	cruelty
being responsible and self-disciplined	irresponsibility

A just and effective society is based on the assumption that certain rules are accepted by most members of the society. These rules reflect shared beliefs and values. Children come to learn that there are reasons for rules and consequences for themselves and others in infringing the rules of a community. The trouble with moral rules such as the ones above is that life constantly throws up situations where what is right and wrong is not universally agreed. It is in the interpretation of these, and other common values such as freedom and fairness, that disputes occur. As one child protested when regularly outvoted by his two brothers, 'Why is it better for two people to be selfish than one?'

Rules may be interpreted differently by different people, and sometimes allowances are made for people who break rules and sometimes not. Who is to decide how rules apply? While values may be shared their sources (religious or secular) vary. In a plural society an acceptance of plurality and diversity of views should be foremost among shared values in a democratic society. This does not mean that children need not hold strong and justified convictions. In the face of competing viewpoints they need to develop for themselves a set of socially acceptable values and principles as guidelines for their own behaviour, while realising that others may have different values and opinions. They need to develop a set of guiding beliefs that will help them to make their own minds up on the range of problems and decisions they will face in life. As Amarjit, age 10, said: 'Things are only frightening when you don't know what to think or do, and you feel alone.'

This book offers starting points for thinking and discussion about values. The values listed as themes in this book are only a selection of the virtues, principles and beliefs, or values for living, that we may wish to explore with our children. They are values for living which have proved to be common aims in a range of schools, expressed in positive terms as a possible focus for reflection and discussion. The list is not exhaustive, and experience shows that there are many more personal, moral and social issues that will arise from the stimulus material of stories and pictures. Children should be encouraged to find their own issues and values to discuss from each starting point, and to reflect on what this means for them and for others. As Amarjit, aged 10, said about Values lessons: 'This is a time when you are not told what to think. You have to work it out for yourself, and its not easy.'

Values for living

The values which provide themes for thinking in this book include:

ambition, caring, co-operation, courage, courtesy, curiosity, empathy, fairness, forgiveness, freedom, friendship, generosity, helpfulness, honesty, ideals, imagination, justice, love, loyalty, modesty, patience, peace, respect for the environment, respect for others, respect for the law, responsibility, self control, sharing, thoughtfulness, toleration, wisdom.

How should we teach values?

'Just giving people rules to follow doesn't make them good.'
Jemma, aged 10.

Moral values are not just about what we do and the rules we follow, they are also about, as Jemma suggests, the sort of people we are, and the goodness (or virtue) that lies within us.

How do we help children to develop a conscience informed by principles which are rationally understood ('I know what I should do') and virtues, such as caring and courage, which provide the disposition to act on judgements ('I know what I would do')?

The building of an individual moral conscience and a strong, resilient inner life is best achieved by means of:

- *example*: models of values in action
- *discussion*: shared enquiry and discussion of moral values, issues and problems
- *encouragement*: support for thinking about, and acting on, value beliefs

Children need to learn from examples and models of values in action, to have opportunities to engage in discussion about moral problems, and to be encouraged to take responsibility for their thoughts and actions. They need to compare their values and beliefs with others and identify common ground. They need to appreciate that distinguishing right and wrong is not always straightforward, that there is a need to examine evidence and reasons before coming to conclusions. They need support to enable them to discuss differences, make informed choices and resolve conflicts. To help in the process of articulating values and beliefs their thinking needs to be informed by awareness of moral ideas and concepts. As one child struggling to explain himself put it: 'I know what I mean, I just don't know the words to describe it.'

Personal, moral, social and citizenship education needs to be taught through exploring values in other subjects across the curriculum as well as in specific values lessons such as Values for Thinking lessons.

1 Values across the curriculum

Values are not separate from the curriculum but are part of all we teach, and are expressed in how we teach. Teaching and learning in all subjects can offer opportunities for promoting the school's values and ethos and developing children's self-confidence and sense of responsibility, developing relationships, working co-operatively with others and reflecting on their own learning and how it relates to living in the wider community. Values permeate all educational activity and all subjects in the curriculum.

The following identify some examples of ways values can occur, and how thinking about values can be promoted in all curriculum areas:

- *English*: use of stories, poems and role play that illustrate personal, moral and social values; exploring other points of view; developing skills in enquiry and communication
- *maths*: co-operation; problem solving; developing financial capability
- *science*: health; sex education; drugs; safety and the environment
- *technology*: human needs; the quality of life; use of technology; health and safety

- *ICT/computers*: use of email and internet; value of information, truth and relevance
- *history*: value of sources; reasons for events; diversity of beliefs, ideas and experiences
- *geography*: environmental issues; other cultures; land use; sustainable development
- *art and design*: values communicated through art, craft and design from different cultures
- *music*: values and cultural diversity expressed in music and in music-making
- *physical education*: health and safety, personal and social skills, fair play in sport
- *religious education*: religious and moral beliefs, values and practices

It is not sufficient to rely solely on these links across the curriculum. Specific provision needs to be made for teaching personal, moral, social and citizenship education separately from other subjects, for example through citizenship days, school councils, circle time, enterprise and charity fundraising schemes, school assemblies and class activities including planned lessons to promote thinking about values.

2   *Values lessons*

Separate curriculum time for thinking about values enables clear planning, identifiable provision and easier monitoring of what is being taught and learnt. A range of teaching strategies is needed to provide breadth of learning opportunities. These include an emphasis on active learning, enquiry, discussion and decision-making in a range of settings, including individual, group and whole class work.

Ways to begin stimulating thinking and discussion of values in specific lessons include the use of:

- dilemmas
- pictures for thinking
- news items
- open questions
- outside visitors
- stories for thinking

Dilemmas

We all face dilemmas in life where we have difficult choices to make. Ask your children if they know what a dilemma is. Illustrate what it means by sharing a dilemma you have faced in life. Ask them if they can give an example of a dilemma (or difficult choice) they have faced in their own lives.

Give them a dilemma to discuss. Encourage them to think about the dilemma from different points of view. Present them with dilemmas faced by different sorts of people. Here for example are dilemmas faced by three different kinds of people. In pairs, and then as a group, ask the children to discuss and give advice on how to resolve these dilemmas:

Moral dilemmas

1 A child's dilemma
The crowd you have always wanted to be in with offer to include you in their number, on condition that you drop your long-time best friend. What do you do?

2 A parent's dilemma
You are a parent. You have a 14 year old son (or daughter) who tells you that his/her best friend is taking drugs. What do you do?

3 A teacher's dilemma
You are a teacher. A child in your class accuses another child from stealing from him/her. The other child says she is being falsely accused (deliberately set up). No one has else any information about the matter. What do you do?

The aim in using dilemmas is to encourage children to be flexible in their thinking, to see problems from different viewpoints and to make carefully considered choices. Follow-up questions can include: 'Are some dilemmas easier to decide on than others?' 'If you have to make a choice, who can help you to decide?' 'What dilemmas have you faced in your life?'

Real-life dilemmas of course face us with many of our most important decisions. It is interesting to note that when Kohlberg was researching the use of dilemmas in assessing children's moral development he came to believe that real-life dilemmas were more fruitful in getting responses from children than fictitious examples. In discussing a real-life dilemma, such as the child who found a £5 note on the way to school and wondered what to do, it can be helpful to consider three key questions: What could you do? What should you do? What would you do?

Pictures

Pictures provide an immediate sensory stimulus. Choose pictures from newspapers, magazines or reproductions of works of art that vividly portray a human situation. The aim is to help children find something meaningful, of value, in the picture and to maximise their capacity for responding to, interpreting and discussing the values in visual material.

Questions to ask about any picture of a human situation include:
- What can you see/what is happening in the picture?
- Who do you think the people, or the person is, in the picture?
- What do you think the person is feeling? Why?
- What do you think they are thinking? Why?
- What are they hoping (will happen)? Why?
- What is strange, interesting or puzzling about this picture?
- What title could you give this picture? Why?

Pictures, including moving pictures such as video or film clips, are useful not only in providing complex objects of intellectual enquiry but also as sources of emotional understanding to encourage empathy and the understanding of others so essential for developing emotional intelligence. One way to start is to look at human faces expressing emotions (see p 57). Show the picture to children. Ask them to identify what emotion(s) the face in the picture might be showing. What might have caused the emotion? Do you remember feeling like that? Why?

Collect and display your own pictures for thinking. Some teachers display a Picture for Thinking each week in their classroom, with a blank sheet alongside it for children to record their questions and comments about the picture. These are then shared and discussed at the end of the week. Pictures for thinking in this book can be found on pp 38, 54, 57 and 113.

News items

Newspapers provide good starting points for the discussion of values. Look at the news stories in today's newspaper. What are the social and moral problems in the news stories? Choose a story relevant to children's life and concerns. Share the story with them. Ask them to identify questions, problems and issues from the story. Use their comments and questions as a stimulus for discussion in a Community of Enquiry (see below). Such discussion should show that real life is a complex affair, that there are many viewpoints to take account of, and that rarely are choices clear-cut. Recognising the plurality of viewpoints, and developing the self confidence to take your own reasoned view, are key aims of such discussion.

Here are some examples of classroom themes for discussion with children prompted by recent stories in the news:

News story	Theme	Key questions
A racist murder	Racism	Why does it occur? Why is it wrong? What can be done about it?
Protests over foxhunting	Animal rights	Why are animals hunted? Should it be allowed?

News of a civil war	War	Why are there wars? What are the alternatives?
Drug-smuggling	Drugs	What are drugs? Is drug-taking bad? Why?
Children not in school	School	Should going to school be compulsory? Why?

(For further ideas on discussing news see 'Newswise' in Further Reading below)

One story for thinking from news of the past is presented on p 107. Are there issues in the news today that mirror problems from the past? As one teacher observed: 'If they do not learn from the past and the present our children will repeat the errors of the past and present.' Many teachers find there is no easier way into citizenship education than involving children in discussing specific issues and problems current in the news. From the local or national newspapers take cuttings of incidents and ask pupils to question the story: What is the story about? What is the main issue/value/problem presented in the story? What happened? Why did it happen? Who is to blame? What could (or should) have been done, or should be done next? What are their views of right and wrong in the story?

Open questions

Open questions can be as fruitful as dilemmas in stimulating discussion and argument. These can be generated from news items in the papers or on TV, from the lives of children (for example having a 'problem' or 'help box' where children can anonymously post problems for later discussion), or from open questions of a general nature.

Examples of open questions to stimulate discussion include:
- What is bullying? What should be done about it?
- Is it more important to be rich or happy?
- Is it better to be an adult or child?
- Are boys and girls treated differently? Should they be?
- What is a hero? Who are your heroes? Why?
- What are laws? Why are they needed? (Create a set of laws for a fictitious society.)
- What are rights? Do children have rights? What should they be? (See Appendix 2)

In one class the teacher asked her class to debate the question 'Should children be smacked if they are naughty?' Here are excerpts from two views children wrote in response to the question after a class discussion:

Should children be smacked when they are naughty?

I don't think they should. Some people say that smacking a child is all right because it makes them remember what they did wrong. But I don't think so. Smacking a child just makes them angry and they forget what they did wrong in the first place. I was smacked once and can't even remember what I did. I think the purpose of punishment is to make the child realise they were wrong and shouldn't do it again. There are lots of better punishments, for instance no pocket money or no sweets for a week ... Another reason why smacking is bad is that it can make the child violent herself. So she goes and smacks someone else. Then that makes them naughty, so I don't think it really works. (Andrea, aged 10)*

I think it is alright to smack children if they have done something really naughty. My brother kicked the cat and was told not to. He did it again and got a smack from my mum. He didn't do it again. Its better to have a smack than be moaned at all the time... (Darren, aged 10)*

Outside visitors

Asking children to question an outside speaker can provide good starting points for thinking about and discussing values. For example, invite local religious leaders to discuss the values embedded in their beliefs and traditions. Ask the children, individually or in groups, to create a questionnaire (it can be helpful to an outside speaker to send these questions beforehand). Discuss the difference between an open and a closed question. Examples of open questions might include: 'Why have their beliefs and traditions lasted so long?' 'Are they changing?' 'How do their beliefs affect the way they live?'

The advantages of using outside speakers include their specialist knowledge (for example of the law or of faith communities), their links with the local community groups and organisations, and their knowledge of real people and situations. Visiting speakers could be people from local agencies such as police, local government or health agencies, or voluntary organisations like charities or religious groups. Meeting people from a variety of work situations, cultures and backgrounds gives children the chance to deepen their knowledge and understanding of values and citizenship. It also provides them with opportunities to develop skills in questioning and discussion, as well as promoting their ability to make positive relationships (through for example writing letters of invitation and thanks).

Stories for Thinking

Stories have been used in every culture and faith to stimulate thinking and to communicate messages and meanings. A good story offers a complex object for intellectual enquiry and may reveal many layers of meaning. An example of a teaching story which is also a mystery is the zen story below.

The Gift of Insults

There once lived a great warrior. Though quite old, he still was able to defeat any challenger. His reputation extended far and wide throughout the land and many students gathered to study under him.

One day an infamous young warrior arrived at the village. He was determined to be the first man to defeat the great master. Along with his strength, he had an uncanny ability to spot and exploit any weakness in an opponent. He would wait for his opponent to make the first move, thus revealing a weakness, and then would strike with merciless force and lightning speed. No one had ever lasted with him in a match beyond the first move.

Much against the advice of his concerned students, the old master gladly acepted the young warrior's challenge. As the two squared off for battle, the young warrior began to hurl insults at the old master. He threw dirt and spat in his face... For hours he verbally assaulted him with every curse and insult known to mankind. But the old warrior merely stood there motionless and calm. Finally the young warrior was exhausted. Knowing he was defeated, he left feeling shamed.

Somewhat disappointed that he did not fight the insolent youth, the students gathered around the old master and questioned him. "How could you endure such insults? How did you drive him away?"

"If someone comes to give you a gift and you do not receive it," the old master replied, "to whom does the gift belong?"

Such stories invite us to reflect on and question their meaning, and to ask, for example:

- What does the story mean?
- What is strange, interesting or puzzling about this story?
- What is the message for me in the story?

The value of using stories is that they are a safe distance from our own pressing concerns and problems, yet provide an opportunity to explore human issues, problems and values which are relevant to us all. We might for example wish to explore the nature of honesty with children through stories such as Aesop's fables 'The Boy Who Cried Wolf' or 'Mercury and the Axe' (*First Stories for Thinking* p 44), or folk tales such as 'The Emperor's New Clothes' by Hans Anderson or 'Not True' (*Stories for Thinking* p 106), or a legend such as 'The Pied Piper of Hamelin', or true historical accounts such as the story of Galileo, or poems such as 'Matilda' by Hilaire Belloc, or stories in this book such as 'The Bishop's Candlesticks' by Victor Hugo (p 63).

Having discussed the story at a literal level, we might wish to explore the values and concepts in the story by discussing the questions children pose (see 'Creating a Community of Enquiry' below) or preparing a discussion plan of our own, such as the following example of questions about honesty.

Thinking about honesty: a discussion plan

Key question: What is honesty

1   What does it mean to be honest?

2   Does everyone tell lies? Is anyone entirely honest?

3   Have you ever told a lie? Why? How did you feel about it?

4   Has anyone lied to you? Give an example. Why did they lie?

5   Why do people tell lies? Can you tell if something is a lie?

6   Is it ever right to tell a lie?

7   What is a 'white lie?' Can you give an example?

8   Are some kinds of lies worse than others? Give examples.

9   Does it take courage sometimes to tell the truth? Give an example.

10   'Honesty is the best policy' is a saying. What does it mean? Do you believe it? Why?

The discussion of a thinking story can provide the groundwork for further creative activity. After a story and discussion about honesty children could, for example:

- Write a story or peom about a 'lie' (eg by putting a lie in every line).
- Read a poem about honesty such as 'What kind of liar are you?' by Carl Sandburg, and write their own thoughts on the poem.
- List some strange facts (eg from the *Guinness Book of Records*) that are true and false. Test them on others. Can they sort fact from fiction?
- Discuss a group of adverts and assess their claims in terms of honesty. Can you detect lies? Tell each other two stories, one true and one a tall story. Can the audience tell the difference?

In a Stories for Thinking lesson children share a story stimulus and are encouraged to raise questions about whatever issues and values they think are relevant to each story in the format known as 'Community of Enquiry'.[2] The stimulus for thinking and discussion is a narrative text or picture. The thirty stories and pictures in this book, linked to thirty or more values, are derived from research with teachers and children in schools. They have all been tried and tested in the classroom and found to be successful starting points for questioning and discussion.[3] The following are the range of texts and pictures included in this book:

- picture
- photo
- poem
- song
- folktale
- myth
- religious story
- legend
- fiction
- factual account

Each picture or story is linked to two discussion plans of sample questions, the first analysing what the story means, the second analysing one of the moral values that relate to the story. This is not meant to suggest that the value (and accompanying discussion plan and activities) is the only value that could be, or should be, questioned and discussed. It offers a suggested model for discussion that could be used. Each value is a key concept that can be connected and related to many other associated concepts. For example when a teacher asked her class of nine year olds to make a concept map about the word 'care' her class linked the word 'care' to the following: 'kindness', 'caring for others', 'caring for yourself', 'caring for the environment', 'looking after', 'showing concern', 'being thoughtful', 'doing good to somebody or something', 'being there when someone needs you', 'clearing up someone's mess', and 'sharing someone's troubles'.

The materials provide a stimulus for discussion and children will find their own issues to discuss from each starting point. The value of a story or picture is that it can provide a safe context for children to raise real issues of moral concern. For example one class who were discussing 'Solomon and the Baby' (p 131) were keen to focus on the issue of 'missing fathers', and the burden of mothers looking after their children alone, relating their own experiences to this scenario. Another class stimulated by 'The Troll's Share' (p 60) discussed the question: 'What shouldn't you share?' which prompted discussion of recent issues in the news about whether people with Down's Syndrome should be refused transplants by the National Health Service, and about the rights of parents to decide whether or not their children should have operations.

The stories and activities in this book provide opportunities to engage children in discussing a range of moral values. Through discussion children will be able to build on their knowledge and understanding of values as a basis for making more thoughtful judgements on moral issues and dilemmas. It also provides a chance for children to question what they do not understand. During discussion of 'What is Better than Gold?' (p 41) Cathy, aged 8, said of 'care': 'Caring is the feeling of love you get when you help someone.' Jody added: 'When you love them and respect them.' Patrick then asked: 'What does 'respect' mean?'

This discussion took place in a 'Community of Enquiry'. A Community of Enquiry is a method of discussing and reasoning about how we should live and what to believe in, which embodies the principles of thinking for oneself and being open to the thinking of others, showing how conflict of opinion can be resolved through thoughtful discussion. A Community of Enquiry gives children the experience of democratic values in action. Through participating in a Community of Enquiry children learn how to reason, to question and to discuss, thereby cultivating the social habits as well as the skills and confidence required for good moral conduct.

Creating a Community of Enquiry

A Community of Enquiry is an ideal way for children to participate in discussion of moral values, as well as to develop the skills of communication and enquiry. Through participating in serious and sustained discussion about issues of importance children develop the skills and confidence that will enable them to play their full part in a pluralistic democratic society. It can boost their self-esteem and intellectual confidence. It does this by creating a caring classroom community where children learn to:

- explore issues of personal concern such as friendship, bullying and fairness, and more general philosophical issues such as love, truth and justice
- develop their own moral viewpoints, and explore and challenge the views of others
- be clear in their thinking, making thoughtful judgements based on reasons
- listen to and respect each other and experience quiet moments of thinking and reflection
- develop skills of reasoned discussion in a democratic setting

Philosophical enquiry initiates children into public discussion about meanings and values. It encourages them to think what it means to be reasonable and to make moral judgements. Such discussions are not just 'talking shops' but help to create a moral culture, a way of thinking and acting together that cultivates virtues of conduct such as respect for others, sincerity and open-mindedness. In a Community of Enquiry children are encouraged to find their own path to meaning via discussion with others. As parents and teachers we cannot control what our children will think or their response to the dangers and temptations they will face on the streets and in their private lives. We can however try to establish a safe place in which to share what they think, feel and experience, and in which their thoughts will be heard. One class calls their 'Values for Thinking' time their Thinking Circle. John, aged 9, commented: 'The Thinking Circle is the only time in school when you really say what you think, and you can change your mind.'

A community of philosophical enquiry provides a safe space for thinking, and a creative context for moral discussion with children of any age or ability. During a discussion of 'The Ten Pound Note' (p 125) when the teacher asked: 'What is thoughtfulness?' a six-year old replied: 'Thoughtfulness is thinking about other people's feelings or helping people like when someone gets hurt in the playground.'

In the process of enquiry and discussion children practise those key skills which enhance the quality of learning and of life. They are encouraged to:
- probe their understanding of the values that underpin belief and action
- learn how to ask relevant questions
- build concepts and argue a case
- detect assumptions and intentions
- develop inferences and hypotheses
- value reasons and recognise faulty reasoning
- gain confidence in their ability to make sense of and to share their values.

The concept of Community of Enquiry is not new, nor is it unique to philosophy for children. Various forms of 'circle time' have been developed to create a supportive environment in which to explore feelings and build self-esteem. A Community of Enquiry is a kind of circle time approach aimed at improving the quality thinking as well as the expression of feeling. But how does this community foster moral development?

In a democracy a community develops by adapting to the individual needs of its members. Decisions in a democracy should always be open to review and reason. The process of democracy ensures this openness to change in response to the needs of individuals through embodying the rights of all to a voice and a vote.

The elements of a democratic community are that it:
- embodies as a principle the freedom of expression of individuals
- makes critical reasoning, not convention, the arbiter of moral judgment
- is organic in the sense that its working procedures and values are open to adaptation
- is democratic in ensuring that all its members have a right to a voice and a vote.

Discussion plays a central role in the development of a community. Learning to talk face to face with other members of one's community about questions of common interest is one of the most basic and important of human activities. For children it not only lays the groundwork for language and literacy development, it also boosts confidence in oneself as a member of a learning community. Good communication and discussion are at the heart of any successful community, whether it be a class, a club or a family. Shared discussion helps to create and sustain the community, and also to solve community problems. Carol, aged 11, summed up the value of democratic discussion by saying: 'A democracy is when everyone has a chance to say what to do to solve a problem, and it's not just left to a few.'

The problem with any community, particularly a pluralist community where individuals come from different cultures and backgrounds, is that there may be many significant and potentially conflicting interests and opinions. Similarly, under the description of democracy there may be many differences of interpretation and practice. Not everyone has the same understanding and experience of life, or of democracy. What is needed is an engagement from an early age in practices that support democracy and the development of understanding of problems and conflicts in life through shared discussion. If children are to learn how to negotiate and make decisions they must engage in practices that support negotiation and decision making. The Community of Enquiry provides just such a forum of careful listening, constructive argument and collaborative discussion where individuals, whether they be children or adults, can find their own path to personal meaning and shared values. As Peter, aged 8, said: 'I have a lot of ideas but I don't get much to say them except in our 'philosophy' lesson.'

The 'philosophy' lesson that Peter mentions is an approach known as Philosophy for Children.[4] It is an approach that underpins the 'Stories for Thinking' series.[5] The following summarises the elements of the Philosophy for Children approach to developing a community of enquiry through discussion in the classroom:

What is a Community of Enquiry?

A Community of Enquiry is a teaching method that includes the following elements:

- *community setting*: sit so all can see and hear each other, with the teacher as part of the group, for example in a horseshoe shape or circle
- *agreed rules*: for example 'Only one speaks at a time', 'Everyone listens to the speaker' – these rules are discussed, agreed and if necessary published for all to see and remember
- *shared stimulus*: each has a turn to read, and the option not to read, a chosen text or to respond to a chosen stimulus for thinking such as a picture or video
- *thinking time*: time is given to think about what is read, or what others say – silent thinking time is encouraged as part of the group's reflective practice

- *questioning*: students are asked to suggest their own questions, or ideas for discussion, which are written for all to see; the group choose one to discuss
- *discussion*: each has a right and opportunity to express their own opinions and feelings and each must listen to others, and consider different views and ideas
- *review*: at the end of the discussion students review the discussion, their own thinking, the views and ideas of others and what they have learnt
- *activities to extend thinking*: activities and exercises may be used to extend thinking about a key issue, developing skills of self expression through art, drama, and creative expression.

A Community of Enquiry has both a cognitive and a moral dimension. The moral dimension is shown by the values we model during the process of enquiry. Learning to listen to and respect the opinions of others models the notion of caring for others, or empathy, that is central to the values of many schools. Of equal moral importance is the notion of thinking for oneself or autonomy, and a third key value is that of justice or fairness, and the protection of rights for all. These values can be both modelled and developed through discussion in the classroom.

Discussing values

Children learn much from the example set by parents and teachers. In our care and teaching of children we need to model those values we think are important. In our discussion with children we need to be consistent in our behaviour, for example to:

- encourage participation by valuing and appreciating the contributions of all children
- display patience and listen seriously and carefully to what they say
- build on ideas and help them to deal with difficult issues
- expect them to give reasons for what they believe and say
- ensure that all honour the group's agreed rules for discussion

Community setting

We should aim to create a peaceful, relaxed but focused climate for discussion. All participants should be able to see each other and to make eye contact when speaking. A circle, or near equivalent setting arrangement such as a horseshoe, allows for this and models equality of position in the group. It also allows for the initial stimulus, such as story, poem or picture to be shared in the most open and accessible way. 'A thinking circle is good', says Gavin, aged 9, 'because no-one is more important than anyone else.'

Agreed rules

Children new to this way of working may find it difficult to sustain reasoned discussion in a group. A good way to start is to agree some rules for the discussion beforehand. In a community of enquiry the rules of a discussion are as important as the content of discussion, for children learn as much by example, and through participating in the discussion, as they do by the discussion of moral concepts. If civilised discussion is a lived experience its rules and conventions will become internalised. Initially however these rules may need to be clearly specified. As Rebecca, aged 8, said: 'I think we need rules to help us remember what it is all about.'

Rules should be few in number, succinct and catchy, and expressed in the fewest number of words possible. They should be negotiated with the children, by asking them for example to develop a set of rules in a small group then for the groups to share with the class. What rules do we agree on? What words best express these rules? Research shows that rules will be more memorable if they are positively phrased. The agreed rules should be clearly displayed in the classroom for easy reference. They should be flexible and open for re-negotiation. They should be teachable and enforceable. The group may need to be frequently reminded of them, and they need to be modelled through the routines of discussion. One way to keep a focus on the rules is to say that anyone can interrupt the discussion if a rule is being broken. A particular child could be given the responsibility for monitoring the discussion to see if the rules are being kept (sometimes an 'unruly' child can be a keen enforcer of group rules if given that responsibility).

Having a set of ground rules can be helpful if you need to challenge a child's contribution to the discussion, for example if they make an inappropriate (such as racist or sexist) remark. If such remarks have been made and are not challenged by other children during the enquiry, then you need to challenge the remark and say why. Check that students understand your reasoning and refer to the ground rules eg 'Our rule is to "respect others", does that comment show respect ...?'

Remind them that if you have agreed the rules they must abide by them. Insist that your agreed rules are followed, in particular the principle that only one person speaks at a time. Remind them they have the right to be silent but an obligation to listen.

Ground Rules

Some rules negotiated by a class of 11 year olds:
- Listen to what other people say
- Be kind to each other and give support
- Think before you speak or ask a question
- Be polite, and don't laugh at what other people say
- Respect others – if people don't want to say anything they don't have to

Shared stimulus

Once the setting of the thinking circle is established and the ground rules agreed, the lesson is launched with a stimulus for thinking. Many teachers like to begin with a warm-up activity or thinking game that will act as a focus or initial stimulus for thinking (see *Games for Thinking* in this series for examples of warm-up activities).

The stimulus for discussion will usually be an object of intellectual enquiry such as story, poem or picture. Each child should be able to clearly see this (for example by showing it to the class on an OHP, enlarging into a 'big book' format or transcribing it onto a large sheet of paper), or have their own copy of the stimulus.

If it is a story it is usually read around the group with each person reading a paragraph. Those who cannot, or do not wish to read, may say 'Pass'. The story is read again, perhaps silently by the children, to allow them time to think carefully about it. Much stress today is laid on the importance of pace in teaching. A 'thinking' lesson may have pace and variety, but it is characterised by something even more important, and something we all need when confronted by complexity and challenge – periods of sustained reflection or thinking time.

Thinking time

Teachers will invite children to think about and to question the story or stimulus. This can be done in various ways. One teacher says to her 6/7 year-olds: 'Can you think of one question or comment about this story?' Another asks: 'Is there anything strange, interesting or puzzling about this story?' A teacher of 10 year-olds poses the question: 'What is the burning issue for you in this story?'

Allow time for children to sit in silence to think through their own thoughts. These could be shared with a partner, then their questions or comments shared with the whole group. Build in thinking time in before the discussion, for children to create their questions, include it during the discussion when you want all the class to think about or respond to a particular point or issue, and at the end of the session in a review or 'last words' time. Emphasise the point that our first thoughts are not always our best thoughts, hence 'thinking again' and 'what do we think now' are useful ways to encourage and sustain thinking.

Thinking time, or 'wait time', can be built in throughout the discussion. Research shows that allowing students 3-5 seconds thinking time after you have asked a question tends to result in children giving better, longer and more elaborate answers, and it also gives them more chance to question what they do not understand. Children learn a lot through example. If we want thinking children we need to model thoughtfulness as teachers or parents. If something is of interest or value it is worth stopping to think about. 'Stop and think' should be our motto (and maybe something to display in the class). We need to stop and think about children's questions and comments, again for about 3-5 seconds, when what they say is worth thinking about. As Trudy, aged 10, said: 'I do my best thinking when I have a chance to stop and think not when I'm rushing on to do the next thing all the time.'

Questioning

Ask children to think of their own questions or comments about the stimulus, at first individually, then in pairs (Did they think of the same question as their partner?) and then shared as a group. Record their questions or comments on a board, large sheet of paper or OHP. Write the name of the name of the child alongside their question, to record and recognise the value of their contribution to the enquiry.

The following are some of the twenty two questions raised from a Year 3 class of 7/8 year olds about 'The Troll's Share' (p 60):

Was the farmer fair? (Natasha)

Who was being greedy? (Nathan)

Who was being selfish? (Ben)

Was the bargain fair? (Lucy)

If the farmer had thought it through could he have come up with something fairer? (Max)

If you were a troll what would you feel like? (Laurie)

Did the troll need three heads? (Ellie)

If you were the troll what would you say or do to the farmer? (Rachel)

How did the troll feel when he had all the useless crop parts? (Melissa)

If you were the farmer would you feel sorry for the troll? (Natasha)

Do you think the troll could have come up with a fairer idea? (Emma)

Do you think they liked each other? (Lucy)

After the class have created and recorded their agenda of questions about the story or picture, ask students to reflect on the questions and to clarify anything they do not understand about any of the questions. Compare and contrast questions. Consider any connections between questions. Think about what kinds of questions they are, and whether they fall into broad categories. Which are good questions? What makes a good question?

One question is chosen to begin the discussion, usually by the class voting for what they think is the most interesting, puzzling or curious question. In the above example Rachel's was the question chosen for discussion. A system of simple majority voting is usual to begin with, but variety can be encouraged later, for example more than one vote per person, one participant or group to choose a question, or a question to be chosen at random.

Discussion

The role of the teacher is to focus the group's attention on the question or issue under discussion, and to push for depth by posing further questions, asking for reasons and evidence, and presenting alternative viewpoints. The aim is to encourage serious, systematic and sustained attention on the question or issue in hand. Asking open or Socratic questions (see below) is one way to probe thinking but alternatives to questions can be just as effective in challenging and extending thinking.

Strategies to extend thinking

- *Wait time*

Remember 'wait time 1 and 2'. Provide at least three seconds of thinking time, after a question and after a child's response.

- *Think-pair-share*

Allow individual thinking time, discussion with a partner, then share and discuss with the class.

- *Ask for more*

Make a non-verbal invitation eg nod of head, sustain them by echoing what they say eg 'So you think that...' or ask them to say more eg 'Can you say more about/give an example...?'

- *Withhold judgement*

Respond in a non-judgemental way eg 'Thank you', 'That's interesting', 'I wonder who agrees/ disagrees?' Cue alternatives eg by asking: 'Who has an alternative view?'

- *Play devil's advocate*

Speculate on the topic and offer a different viewpoint eg by saying: 'I wonder what would happen if ...'

- *Make a personal contribution*

Offer information or an example from your own experience eg by saying 'I remember when...'

- *Invite their further questions*

Encourage questioning during discussion, by asking for example: 'Has anyone a question to ask?' 'What do we still need to think about?'

In a Values for Thinking lesson the challenge for the teacher is to help the group focus on the moral questions and underlying values of issues being discussed. One teacher summed this up by saying: 'My task is to get children to realise there are moral choices to be made, and that they must have good reasons for what they think and say.'

Begin by asking the questioner why they asked the question. Try to establish the main views relating to the question at the outset. Ask who agrees or disagrees with what is said. Encourage participants to speak to each other, and to look at the speaker, rather than the teacher. Try to focus the discussion on the chosen question, but allow references to related questions and issues if appropriate.

With young children judgements about right and wrong are invariably made in terms of self interest. What discussion can do is to help them understand the idea of things being right or wrong for reasons other than self interest – for example the consequences for others. They can also be helped to see the relevance of abstract moral principles to real situations, such as the Golden Rule, 'Only do to others only what you would wish them to do to you'.

The capacity for moral reasoning develops at different rates in individuals. Many secondary pupils seem stuck in the belief that things are wrong simply because 'you can get in trouble for it', and that cheating is right 'if you can get away with it'. What discussion can do is to present pupils with a range of different viewpoints and grounds for judging why something may be right or wrong. Without the challenge of such discussion, human beings at whatever age may remain trapped in what Socrates called their 'unconsidered' lives, in accepting what others have told them or their own lazy assumptions. As Donna, aged 11, said: 'Until you really discuss things you think everyone thinks the same.'

In discussing a moral issue there may be no right or wrong answers, but there are questions to be raised, opinions to be shared and thinking to be challenged by being exposed to new and different viewpoints. Such discussion should not be just an optional extra to a curriculum (or to a life) but is central to the whole process of educating, and being, thoughtful and responsible citizens.

Why are there good and bad people?

A group of 10 year olds have read 'The Pardoner's Tale' (p 76) and are sitting in a circle discussing Joanne's question: 'Why are there good and bad people?' They are used to this format and listen attentively to each other. A number of different opinions are expressed. No one feels nervous about sharing their own opinions or questioning the opinions of others. There are periods when many want to speak at once, and times of quiet reflection. The teacher guides her students to consider their thoughts in greater depth and to give reasons for their views. Here is an excerpt from that discussion:

CHILD: I think people are basically good and want to do good things.

TEACHER: Anyone agree or disagree with that?

CHILD: I disagree with Jane. I think everyone has bad within them. It is only parents or teachers who make you good.

CHILD: I think we are born good but it is things like television that make you bad. Seeing bad things gives you bad ideas.

CHILD: I think people are both good and bad. There's good and bad in everyone, just waiting to come out really. That's how we are made. You can choose to be good or bad.

continued

TEACHER:	What do you think helps you to be good?
CHILD:	It's your feelings really. If you do good things you feel good.
CHILD:	Sometimes when you do bad things you feel good too!
TEACHER:	Can you give an example of that?
CHILD:	Like taking ice cream when you shouldn't.
CHILD:	I think there is a difference. When you are doing good things for others, like helping an old lady across the road, you are feeling for them. When you do bad and selfish things you are only feeling for yourself ...

Introduce and encourage them to use the vocabulary of discourse, such as 'agree/disagree', 'argument', 'example', 'hypothesis'. Display these words in the classroom.

Reviewing the discussion

If discussing what we think is of value, then what we discuss must be worth serious thought. If the discussion is to be successful then the thinking and reasoning must be valued and trust established. The teacher or discussion leader should also give time for thinking about and reviewing the discussion. Leading a plenary or debriefing session is not an easy task. It is a complex teaching skill characterised by:

- *a high proportion of open or Socratic questions*, such as:
  'Have we discussed anything important today?'
  'What was the most important concept (or idea) that we discussed?'
  'Did we ask any difficult questions (or pose any problems)?'
  'Did anyone have good thoughts or new ideas'
  'Did we have good reasons, arguments or evidence to support what was said?'
  'Did we explain our ideas well?'

- *lengthy pupil responses, encouraged by the teacher*, as in the following excerpt from a review of a discussion by a group of 9 year olds about whether it is right for parents to smack their children:

TEACHER:	Who in the discussion had a good reason for what they said?
CHILD:	I think Sophie's was a good idea why smacking children is wrong.
TEACHER:	What was the idea?
CHILD:	Well she said it was wrong because smacking you doesn't tell you why it was wrong, it just tells you that if you do it you will get smacked. That means you'll do it again if you can get away with it and not be smacked. But if you are told why it is wrong... whatever it is ... then you are less likely to do it again. Because you know why it is wrong. If you understand the reason...'

- *reference by the teacher to the 'big' ideas or concepts* under discussion, as in the following way a teacher links a particular point to a broader concept:

TEACHER: When you say people should not tell lies do you mean they should be honest in all circumstances? Why is honesty so important do you think?

- *connecting what is discussed to other topics and everyday life*, as in the following:

TEACHER: We've talked about courage and how it is sometimes difficult to tell other people what we think. Who can give me an example of courage from the history topic we have just been studying?

You may wish to reserve time at the end of the discussion for a round of 'last words' to encourage less active participants to make a contribution. Questions for the group to consider during self-evaluation include:
'What have we learnt?'
'What were the most interesting thoughts and ideas?'
'Has anyone changed their minds (and if so why)?'
'Are there any important issues we have not discussed?'
'Does anyone have a question we should discuss next time?'
'Is there a better way to organise the discussion?'

This kind of oral feedback about what has been discussed can be extended through the use of written review. Here a 7 year old writes her reflections on the story : 'The Talking Turtle' (p 119) that has just been discussed by the class: 'In this story I learnt that you can talk too much. I can control my mouth, but I sometimes go over the top and I use horibal laguage (*sic*). I can control my mouth sometimes if I try.'

Socratic questioning

Socratic questioning means using a series of questions to progressively engage higher levels of thinking – including literal, analytical and conceptual levels of thinking. The following are examples of questions that engage these three levels of thinking:

1   Literal (or factual) questions, which ask for information
'What is this about?'
'Can you remember what happened?'
'What do you have to do?'

2   Analytic questions, which call for critical and creative thinking
'What question(s) do you have?'
'What reasons can you give?'
'What are the problems/possible solutions here?'

3   Conceptual questions, which call for abstract thinking
'What is the key concept (strategy or rule) here and what does it mean?'
'What criteria are we using to judge this (or test if it is true)?'
'How might we further investigate this concept (strategy or hypothesis)?'

Follow-up activities

A number of follow-up activities are suggested at the end of each section to extend thinking about the theme, for example through writing, drawing, or role-play, which may take the form of individual, paired or small group work. For example, after a class had discussed the concept of friendship (p 70) the teacher gave out a number of statements about friendship and asked them to sort the statements into two piles, one for those they agreed with and one for those they disagreed with. Each group then compared their decisions with another group, and then with the whole class.

What is a friend?

Which of these statements do you agree with and which do you disagree with?

A friend is someone who is always there to help when things go wrong.

A friend will always forgive you if you do something wrong.

Friends are just the people you see every day.

Friends are people who are the same race and religion as you.

A friend is someone who does what you say.

A friend is someone who will never lie to you.

A friend is a special person you can share secrets with.

A friend is someone who is loyal to you – no matter what.

Another extension activity might be to make a concept web around the central concept under discussion, or a 'mindmap' of the main points in the discussion. Give students their own 'thinking book', journal or learning log to write and record their reflections after the enquiry. Keep evidence of past enquiries for reference and accessible to all in the classroom.

Assessing moral development

Moral development means enabling children to develop a set of values that are both personal, relating to self interest, and public, relating to the interests of others. A moral judgement must be made freely. A parrot, or young child, repeating 'It is wrong to steal' is not making a moral judgement. A moral judgement must be that person's judgement – it must come from the self. A moral judgement is also inter-personal and it must, if others are equally important, apply to others. Hence insight into oneself and insight into the needs and feelings of others are equally important elements in moral education.

Self

One of the key elements of moral education is *autonomy* – that is, the capacity to think for oneself. It is indicated by evidence of children thinking for themselves, for example in taking a minority viewpoint, or in challenging the viewpoint of others. It shows itself in a developing sense of self esteem, and in the willingness of children to take responsibility for how their lives should be lived. Autonomy can be exemplified in questions such as:

- What do I really think?
- What do I feel about myself (or about the situation)?
- What sort of life do I want to lead?
- What sort of person do I want to be?
- What are my values and my priorities?

Evidence from teachers that indicate a growing sense of autonomy in children include:

'That is the first time I have heard Jasbir volunteer her own opinion.'

'Kirsty showed she was able to self-correct when she changed her mind and corrected her earlier opinion about what it means to be a friend.'

'Paul really showed confidence when he stuck out for his opinion against the others ...'

Others

Another element of moral education is *empathy*, that is the state of being emotionally and cognitively 'in tune' with another person, in particular understanding what their situation is like for them. We show who we are through our sense of self (*autonomy*) and through our relationships with others (*connectedness*). The paradox of human life is that we are both separate as individuals yet connected as part of a culture. Individuals find fulfilment in living relations. Who we are is partly made up of the context that we are in and the relationships we have formed. This dichotomy between self and others is reflected in two views of democracy, one identifying democracy with the freedom of the individual to pursue self interest, the other seeing individuals essentially as creators of communities. In any community there is a tension between the right to freedom and the responsibility towards others. In a Community of Enquiry the right to freedom is shown in two ways, one in freedom of expression (even when you are wrong), the other is the right to silence, to pass, to listen and not to comment. Responsibility to others is shown through caring behaviour.

Caring or empathy requires the exercise of moral imagination, that is the ability to create and rehearse possible situations, to make 'thought experiments' such as putting oneself in the place of another. This sense of interconnectedness, in which children realise they are one among many with interests and desires like others, is a necessary foil to prejudice and to thinking of people as stereotypes. The kinds of questions that exemplify empathy include:

- How would you (or that other person) feel?
- How would I feel if it happened to me (or to you)?
- What would it be like (or would you think) if you were the other person?
- Have I ensured (are we ensuring) equal opportunities for all?
- How do I show others I respect and value them?

Examples of teachers noting evidence of caring behaviour in discussion include:

'Saeed did well to insist that everyone should have a turn to speak.'

'An example of the way Karen shows empathy was when she said, "Imagine what it would be like to be that person".'

'What was significant was the way everyone listened attentively to what others had to say.'

Society and beyond

A third related element is the ability to 'decentre' from the self and those we know, to look at a situation as it were from above, from as objective a viewpoint as we can get, as it were from the point of view of the universe. This refers to the ability to transcend individual or group interest so as to think what would be right for anyone in a given situation, to look beyond the self interest of individuals or groups such as friends and family, and to include the wider society and ultimately a world-view. It is to be conscious of the relationship of human beings not only to each other but to nature, and includes our duties to other species. It is an awareness of the importance of universal principles such as justice or fairness. For some moral theorists, such as Kant and Kohlberg, the highest form of moral reasoning lies in the formulation of universal principles or duties. For others transcendence lies in seeking what is good, right or fair for people in particular situations.

The kinds of questions that exemplify a set of transcending values include:

- What would be the consequences if everyone acted in this way?
- What are the implications of behaving (or believing) that way?
- What is the right thing to do?
- Would it be right in every circumstance?
- What principle, value or moral is involved?

Examples of evidence of awareness of universal moral values include:

'Anne referring to the principle of doing to others as you would have them do to you.'

'I liked the way Kerry said if the rule was right for you it was right for everyone.'

'Paul did not just say it was not fair, he gave a reason why it was a fair rule and in what circumstances it should apply.'

Qualities of a moral person	Principles of moral education	Key question
autonomy	thinking for oneself	What is right for me?
empathy	showing care for others	What is right for others?
transcendence	upholding principles of justice/fairness	What is right for all?

In personal and social education (PSHE) and citizenship there are two broad areas for assessment:

1   Children's knowledge and understanding, for example information on health and safety, and the meaning of key ideas such as democracy.

2   Children's skills and attitudes, for example through participating in discussions, group tasks and activities, managing conflict, making decisions and promoting positive relationships.[6]

There is a clear link between values and the thinking skills which underpin children's understanding and their developing skills and attitudes.

Thinking skills

Thinking skills identified in the rational for the National Curriculum include:

- information processing skills
- questioning skills
- reasoning skills
- creative thinking skills
- evaluating skills[7]

Information processing skills

These enable students to find relevant information; to communicate, compare and contrast information; and to identify and analyse relationships. They help build knowledge and understanding of key concepts of citizenship – such as fairness, justice and democracy. They are developed through investigating and discussing topical issues, problems and events.

Questioning skills

These enable pupils to ask relevant questions; to pose and define problems; to plan, research and predict outcomes; to anticipate consequences and draw conclusions. They develop these skills when they investigate and raise questions about personal, moral and social issues, and the values and institutions that influence their lives. These skills enable pupils to think for themselves and learn from others.

Reasoning skills

These enable students to give reasons for opinions and actions, to draw inferences and make deductions, to use precise language to explain what they think, and to make judgements and decisions informed by reasons or evidence. They are developed through discussion of personal, moral and social issues that require reasoning, argument and explanation. These skills help them to engage effectively in democratic discussion and decision-making.

Creative thinking skills

These enable students to generate ideas, suggest hypotheses, apply criteria in evaluation and use imagination in looking for alternative and innovative outcomes. Citizenship and values education provide opportunities for students to use their imagination in considering other people's experiences and in thinking about other points of view. Pupils develop these skills when they seek innovative answers to questions or solutions to problems.

Evaluation skills

These enable students to evaluate information, to judge the value of what they read, hear and do, and to develop criteria for judging the value of their own or others' work or ideas. They are developed when pupils make informed and reasoned judgements about moral issues such as fairness and community issues such as justice at a local, national and global level. They enable pupils to assess their own judgements and the judgements of others.

The link between thinking skills and moral (and citizenship) education can summed up in the need to encourage imaginative reasoning. As one child said during a discussion: 'Without an imagination you can't draw, you can't read ... without imagination you can't do anything.' Another said: 'Imagination helps us to know what it is like for other people.' The use of imaginative reasoning is necessary if children are come to see themselves not only in relation to others in the present world, but also in the world that *could be*. As one ten year-old put it: 'You need imagination to think how the world might be.'

With the help of a Community of Enquiry children can transcend the present, and be helped through imaginative reasoning to construct an understanding not only of what is but what could be. Participation in a Community of Enquiry aims to give children the tools they need to question what is and to begin the search for constructive ways to change or transform it into what might be. 'We can make a better world,' said Sophie, aged 10, 'the question is "Where do we begin?" '

Notes

[1] For more on ways to develop different forms of intelligence in children see
Fisher, R. (1999), *Head Start: How to Develop Your Child's Mind* (Souvenir Press)

[2] For more on Community of Enquiry see Fisher, R. (1998), *Teaching Thinking: Philosophical Enquiry in the Classroom*, Cassell

[3] The Lessons in Values Education (LIVE) project was a research project conducted by the author with teachers in primary schools in the London area.

[4] For more information on Philosophy for Children contact the Society for Advancing Philosophical Enquiry in Education (SAPERE) www. sapere.co.uk

[5] Other books in the 'Stories for Thinking' programme include
Fisher, R., (1996), *Stories for Thinking*, Oxford: Nash Pollock
Fisher, R., (1997), *Poems for Thinking*, Oxford: Nash Pollock
Fisher, R., (1997), *Games for Thinking*, Oxford: Nash Pollock
Fisher, R., (1999), *First Stories for Thinking*, Oxford: Nash Pollock
Fisher, R., (2000), *First Poems for Thinking*, Oxford: Nash Pollock

[6] QCA (2000), *Personal, social and health education and citizenship at key stages 1 and 2*, p 15

[7] DfEE/QCA (1999), *The National Curriculum. Handbook for primary teachers in England. Key stages 1 and 2*, p 22

Further reading

DfEE/QCA (1998), *Education for citizenship and the teaching of democracy in schools: Final report of the Advisory Group on Citizenship* (Crick Report)

DfEE/QCA (1999), *Citizenship: The National Curriculum for England* www.nc.uk.net

QCA (2000), *Personal, Social and Health Education and Citizenship at Key Stages 1 and 2*

Fisher, R. (1995), *Teaching Children to Think*, Oxford: Blackwell.

Fisher R. (1998), *Teaching Thinking*, London: Cassell.

Fisher R. (1999), *Head Start: How to Develop Your Child's Mind*, London: Souvenir Press

Fisher R. (2000), 'Philosophy for children: how philosophical enquiry can foster values education in schools', in Gardner, R., Cairns J & Lawton D. (2000), *Education for Values*, London: Kogan Page

Goleman D. (1995), *Emotional Intelligence*, London: Bloomsbury

Murris K. and Haynes J. (2000), *Storywise*, www.dialogueworks.co.uk

Rowe D. & Newton J. (1994), *You, Me, Us!: Social and Moral Responsibility in Primary Schools*, London: Citizenship Foundation

Sutcliffe R. & Williams S. (2000), *Newswise*, www.dialogueworks.co.uk

For further information on research and publications contact:

Professor Robert Fisher, Brunel University, 300 St. Margarets Road, Twickenham TW1 1PT.

Website: www. teachingthinking.net

Themes

1 AMBITION

I want! I want!

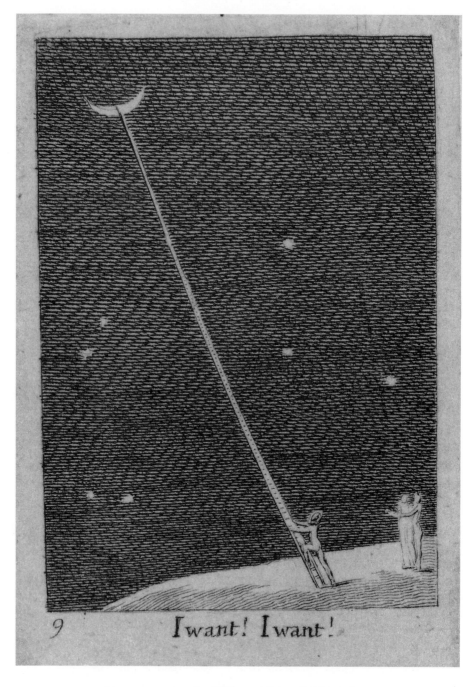

Line engraving by William Blake (1757-1827)

Note: Teachers may make an OHP.

Thinking about the picture

Key question: What does the picture mean?

1 What can you see in the picture?

2 How do you think the picture was made? (Engraved on a steel plate, printed in black ink)

3 What kind of picture do you think it is? (It is a line engraving)

4 What words can you see? Why are they there, do you think? (Title, name of artist, date)

5 Do you think the picture tells a story? What might the story be?

6 Why is he using a ladder? Could you put a ladder to the moon?

7 Does this picture show real life? Why? Is it from imagination? Is it a dream picture?

8 Why is it called 'I want! I want!'?

9 Can you think of another title for this picture?

10 Why do you think the artist created this picture?

Thinking about ambition

Key question: What is ambition?

1 What does it mean to 'want' something?

2 Do we all want things?

3 Do we all want the same things? Why, or why not?

4 Is there a difference between needing and wanting?

5 Do you always need the things you want?

6 Do people sometimes want things that are not good for them?

7 What do you want for yourself in the future? What ambitions have you got?

8 What is an ambition?

9 Is it good to be ambitious? Why?

10 Is it possible to get anything if you want it enough?

Further activities

- List all the ambitions you have in life. Put them in order of preference. Share with others.

- Make a survey of what others most want to be when they grow up.

- Find out as much as you can about the artist William Blake.

- Discuss what the expression 'Reaching for the moon' means.

- Make up a science fiction story about a traveller trying to reach another planet or world

Thought for the day

> 'Ah, but a man's reach should exceed his grasp,
> Or what's a heaven for?'
>
> *(Robert Browning, 'Andrea del Sarto', 98)*

2 CARING

What is Better than Gold?

There was once a King who had three daughters. He was growing old, and began to wonder how much his daughters loved him. So one day he thought he would find out. He sat himself down on his throne in the great hall, and sent for the first of his daughters. She was his eldest. She knew her father very well and she knew what he liked best.

'Now tell me, daughter,' said the King. 'How much do you love me?'

The eldest daughter thought for a moment before she replied, 'I love you more than gold, father.'

The old King smiled. There was nothing he liked more than gold. 'You have spoken well,' said the King.

Next he called for the second daughter and asked her how much she loved him.

'I love you, father, more then silver,' she replied, and her father smiled. He loved the shine of silver, the glint of coins and riches.

'You have spoken well,' said the King.

Finally he sent for the third daughter. She was the youngest, and she loved her father dearly.

'Now tell me, child,' said the King. 'How much do you love me?'

The youngest daughter thought carefully before she answered.

'I love you, father, better than salt.'

The old King blinked. 'Speak again, daughter,' he said. 'I don't think I heard you quite right.'

'I love you, father, more than salt.'

'Salt! Salt is nothing!' roared the King. 'You do not love me at all! Go, and never let me see you again!'

At this the youngest daughter burst into tears and ran from the room. She loved her father very much, but he did not seem to understand. What could she do? Where could she go?

Still crying, she ran downstairs until she came to the palace kitchens.

There the cooks were busy preparing the King's supper. An idea came to her. She ordered the cooks not to add any salt to the King's food, to add no salt to the soup, to put none in the vegetables when they were boiled, to mix none in the sauces, no salt in the gravy, no salt in the butter, no salt in the fish, no salt in the chips.

'No salt at all?' asked the cooks.

'No salt at all,' answered the princess.

So the cooks prepared the food as the princess had ordered. That evening the King sat down to his supper feeling grumpier than usual. His knives and forks were of silver and his plates were of gold. But the King was thinking only of his food. In came the soup. The King tasted it.

'Ugh! Take it away' he said. 'It's got no taste.'

Then came the fish. That too was tasteless. The meat, the vegetables, even the chips – there was something wrong with all of them.

'Fetch me the cooks!' he bellowed.

The cooks came trooping in. The King glared at them.

'Who cooked this dreadful meal?' asked the King.

'Your Majesty,' said the chief cook, 'we just followed the princess's orders. Leave out the salt she said, so we did.'

Slowly the King realised how wrong he had been. He sent at once for his youngest daughter. 'I never knew how important salt was,' he said. 'Please forgive me for being so angry. You love me like salt, and your love is better than silver or gold.'

(European folktale)

Thinking about the story

Key question: What does the story mean?

1   How did the King try to find out if his daughters loved him?
2   Do you think it was a good way of finding out?
3   What did the daughters say?
4   Why was the King angry with the youngest daughter?
5   What idea did the youngest daughter have?

6   Why did the King not enjoy his supper?

7   What did the King slowly realise?

8   What did the King now think was better than silver or gold?

9   What made the King change his mind?

10   What did the King mean, 'You love me like salt'?

Thinking about caring

Key question: What does caring mean?

1   What does caring for someone mean?

2   Do you think caring is a thought or feeling or both?

3   Can you care for someone you do not like? Explain why, or why not.

4   Can you suddenly start, or stop, caring for someone?

5   How do you show you care for someone?

6   Is caring the same as loving?

7   Is it possible to think someone is caring for you when they aren't really?

8   Is it possible to care for someone and they not know it?

9   Who should you care for? Why?

10   Who should care for you? Why?

Further activities

- Listen to a pop song about love. Discuss the lyric.

- Write a group poem with each line beginning: 'Love is ...'

- Find out what you can about gold. What is made of gold? Why is it so precious?

- Read the story of Shakespeare's *King Lear*. How is it similar to or different from this story?

- Cook something special for someone (remember to add some salt!).

Thought for the day

'Greater love hath no man than this, that a man lay down his life for his friends.' (*The Bible, John 15:13*)

3 CO-OPERATION

The Two Metre Chopsticks

Once upon a time in far off China there lived a brave warrior, who met his death in battle, fighting for his country. He had lived a good life. He had been afraid of nothing, not even of the arrow that had pierced his heart. When he died he expected to be laid in one of the cold tombs on the hill. Instead he found himself waiting outside the gates of Heaven.

A man was waiting there ready to receive him. 'Welcome,' he said. 'I was told that you were coming.'

'But where am I?' asked the warrior.

'This is Heaven, of course. The home of the brave and good after they have lived their earthly life.'

'Tell me,' said the warrior, 'where do all the others go?'

'Oh, they go to the other place. Don't worry, you won't be bothered by them.'

'I'd like to see this other place,' said the warrior. 'Take me down to Hell.'

'All right, come with me,' said the guide. 'But you won't like what you see.'

So off they went, and soon arrived at the gates of Hell. Carefully they pushed the gates open. Inside the warrior could see a table, and on this table was a bowl piled high with freshly cooked rice. There were people sitting round the table, but the warrior was amazed to see that they were all starving. They looked thin, and mean, and miserable. The warrior soon saw why. For each person had in his hands chopsticks which were two metres long! Only by using the chopsticks could they reach the rice. But the chopsticks were so long that no matter how much rice they picked up they could never get the food into their mouths. It dropped on their heads, and in their eyes, and all over the floor. There was a terrible mess. Squabbles kept breaking out, food was flying, and the noise was unbearable.

The warrior looked at his guide. 'Can we go back now?' he asked.

So they did. The gates of Heaven opened wide and the warrior was led through. Once in Heaven the warrior was amazed to see the same table as he had seen in Hell, and there was the same bowl piled high with tasty rice, and sitting round the table were people using two metre chopsticks.

The warrior could hardly believe his eyes. 'But this is just what it was like in Hell,' he moaned.

'Really?' said his guide. 'Can't you see any difference?'

The warrior looked again. There was a difference. There were no sad, starving faces here. The people round the table all looked healthy and jolly. They were laughing and munching at the food. How was this possible?

The warrior soon saw the reason why. Instead of each trying to grab what he could for himself, the people in Heaven were helping to feed each other. Although the chopsticks were too long for their own mouths, they were not too long for helping others. Each of them was using his chopsticks to feed someone else.

Now the warrior understood. Heaven and Hell were the same places. It was just that in Hell the people were selfish, and starved, while in Heaven they helped each other, and were happy.

(Chinese folktale)

Thinking about the story

Key question: What does the story mean?

1   How did the warrior die?

2   What did he expect would happen after his death?

3   Where did he find himself after he died?

4   Why did the warrior want to visit Hell?

5   Why were people unhappy in Hell?

6   What did the warrior see in Heaven?

7   Why were the people healthy and happy in Heaven?

8   What do you think the moral of this story is?

9   Are Heaven and Hell the same place in the story?

10   Can you think of examples where people are happy helping each other?

Thinking about co-operation

Key question: What is co-operation?

1   Do you prefer to work with others or by yourself. Why?

2   'Many hands make light work'. What jobs in life are better done with other people?

3   What jobs are better done by yourself? Why?

4   What are the problems about doing things with other people?

5   People sometimes talk of a 'weak link' in a chain. What does that mean?

6   What games require people to co-operate in a team? Which is your favourite? Why?

7   Does every team need a captain, or someone in charge? Why? Give examples.

8   How is a family, a class or a school like a team?

9   How do you get people to co-operate who don't want to? Give an example.

10   Is it always good to co-operate? What things would you not co-operate in doing? Why?

Further activities

• Prepare a meal with each person contributing a dishes. Serve the food to others.

• Work on a large project eg create a communal frieze or tapestry made up of many parts.

• Find a recent newspaper story which illustrates local, national or international co-operation.

• One stick is easily broken. Find out how many put together become unbreakable.

• Create your own co-operative team game. Explain how to play it to others.

Thought for the day

'Unity is strength.'

4 COURAGE

How the Guru chose Five Lions

In a Sikh temple the Holy Book is guarded by five men holding swords. Here is the story of how Guru Gobind Singh chose the first five men to protect the Holy Book. It happened in the year 1699 when the leader of the Sikh people in India, whom they called the Guru, asked all the Sikhs to meet him at a town called Anandpur.

The Guru, with a sword in his hand, stood before the huge crowd.

'I have called you here,' he said, 'to find the bravest of my followers! These I need to guard our Holy Book, and for that only the bravest will do.'

The crowd stirred and wondered who would be chosen. Many of them thought they were brave enough to serve the Guru. But how was he to find out which of his followers was really the bravest? What kind of test would he give them to find out who was brave? The crowd waited for the Guru to speak.

The Guru decided to have a test to find out who the bravest of his followers were. Lifting his sword he asked them, 'Who among you is brave enough to have his head cut off?'

No one moved. Again he asked the question. There was no answer. For a third time he repeated the question, 'Who is prepared to have his head cut off?' There was silence. Suddenly a man spoke. 'I am,' he said. 'I cannot think of a better way of dying.'

As the people watched the man walked forward and followed the Guru into his tent. The sword was heard to fall, and the Guru came out with his sword dripping with blood.

The Guru asked if there was another man prepared to have his head cut off. There was a short pause, then another Sikh stepped forward and disappeared into the Guru's tent. Again the sword was heard to fall, and the Guru appeared with blood dripping from the blade. Then a third man stepped forward, and the same thing happened. A fourth and a fifth man offered their lives and were taken into the tent of death.

After the fifth man entered the tent the Guru appeared once more, still carrying his blood-stained sword. Behind him the tent flap opened and the crowd gasped. They saw something that amazed them. Out of the tent came the five men, alive and unharmed. The Guru had found his five bravest men.

'From this day I will call these men Singh,' said the Guru (Singh means 'lion'), 'for they have proved they are as brave as lions.'

The Guru then told the people that they should all be brothers and sisters, and to show this was only right, that they should share the same name. That way they would remember to be as brave as those five men who were his first 'Lions'.

(Sikh story)

(*Note*: The Guru said that every female Sikh should add the name Kaur after her first name. Kaur means 'princess', showing that women too have a proud and important position among Sikhs.)

Thinking about the story

Key question: what does the story mean?

1   Why did the Guru want to find five brave men?

2   What plan did the Guru have to find the bravest of his followers?

3   What did the crowd think was happening?

4   How many times did he call for volunteers?

5   Why do you think the five men volunteered?

6   What do you think happened inside the tent?

7   What did the Guru call the five men? Why?

8   Why did the Guru ask his followers to share the same name?

9   Why do you think he decided to choose men and not women?

10   What is a Guru?

Thinking about bravery and courage

Key question: What is courage?

1 What does it mean to say someone is being brave?

2 Are only heroes brave or can anyone show courage or bravery?

3 Is being brave about something you do or about how you feel inside?

4 Can you be brave and still be afraid?

5 Do you always know when you are being brave?

6 Who is the bravest person you know? In what way are they brave?

7 Is everyone scared sometimes? What are you scared of?

8 Is it always a good thing to be brave? Why?

9 Courage is said to be a virtue. What is a virtue?

10 When should you be brave? What helps you to be brave?

Further activities

• Courage is a virtue. List other virtues. Discuss their order of importance.

• Discuss common and uncommon fears. Write a poem beginning 'Fear is ...'

• Find and share a newspaper story of someone showing courage.

• Interview someone whose job involves courage eg fireman, lifeboat crew.

• Ask children to recount the bravest thing they ever did.

Thought for the day

'We become brave by doing brave things.'

(Aristotle, 384-322 BCE)

5 COURTESY

The Courtesy of Saladin

During the Crusades the English knights who went out to fight the Arab armies for control of the holy places in Palestine came back with many new things they had seen and learned from their enemies. They brought back with them perfumes and medicines, carpets, Arabic numbers, strange fruits like oranges and apricots, and many stories, including stories of the courtesy of the Arabs. This is one of those stories.

The crusading knights of King Richard the Lionheart had driven the Arab army back into the great walled city of Acre. Inside this great city was Saladin, the chief of the Saracens, and the remains of his once proud Arab army. King Richard and his knights felt very pleased with themselves. They were driving their enemies out of the Holy Land, and now they had their greatest enemy Saladin himself trapped inside the city. But the question was, how were they to get him out? The walls of the city were very thick. Whenever the crusaders came close to the great wooden gates they were driven back by a hail of stones and arrows. There was no way into the city. What could they do? They decided that the only way to win was to starve Saladin into surrender.

So the great army of King Richard camped all round the city and waited. No one was allowed in or out of the city gates. 'They will have to surrender,' thought Richard, 'when their food runs out, and there is no water to drink. The city, and Saladin, will soon be mine.'

The trouble was that King Richard's own men were also short of food, and what was worse, as time went by they began to run out of water. The country around was a desert, the sun scorched down and the rivers were running dry. Day after day the knights sat in their tents sweating under their heavy armour and chain-mail, waiting for Saladin to surrender. But nothing happened. They grew hotter and hotter, and thirstier and more bad tempered. Surely in the city the inhabitants could not survive without supplies of food or water?

What the crusaders did not realise was that inside the city there was a great store of food. Fresh fruit and vegetables were growing in their gardens, the people stayed cool in their houses, and inside the city was a spring of fresh water. Saladin gazed down from the city walls and saw how the crusaders were suffering in the heat. Weeks went by, and still nothing happened. Then one day the great wooden gates of the city slowly creaked open.

Were they surrendering at last? King Richard was called from his tent to look. What he saw surprised him. Through the gates of the city came a cart pulled by two huge oxen. Piled high on the cart were large round things, coloured green. The wooden gates shut again, and the cart rumbled towards King Richard's camp.

'Look out!' shouted one of his knights. 'It might be a trap.'

The crusaders stepped back as the cart moved closer and closer to their tents. Tied to the top of the carts was a message. King Richard called for it to be read to him. It read: 'A gift to King Richard, my honoured guest, by courtesy of Saladin.' The King looked suspiciously at the pile of round green balls.

'Which of my knights will test for me this gift from my enemy?' asked the King.

The knights eyed each other and shifted uneasily in their chain-mail. At last one of them stepped forward. 'I will, Your Majesty,' he said, and very carefully he lifted one of the great balls from the cart. The other knights stepped back. The brave knight took his sword and cut into the skin of the ball. Inside it looked sweet and juicy. Slowly the knight raised it to his lips and sucked. A smile spread across his face and he sucked again. It was cool sweet water tasting of honey. Saladin had sent them a precious gift – a gift of melons!

(Medieval legend)

Thinking about the story

Key question: What does the story mean?

1 What were the English knights doing in Palestine?

2 What did they bring back with them from Palestine?

3 Who was Saladin?

4 Why did King Richard feel pleased that Saladin was in the city of Acre?

5 What problems did King Richard's men face as they waited outside the city of Acre?

6 What did the crusaders not realise as they waited outside the city?

7 What came out of the city that surprised Richard?

8 Why was he worried about the large green balls?

9 Why do you think Saladin sent Richard this gift?

10 Do you think this is a true story? Why? What do you think happened next?

Thinking about courtesy

Key question: What is courtesy?

1 What does 'being polite' mean? Give an example of being polite. What is the opposite of polite?

2 What does being rude mean? Give an example. Why are people rude?

3 Have you ever been rude? Give an example. What did you think then (and now)?

4 Have people been rude to you? Give an example. How did you feel? What did you think?

5 What are good and bad manners? Where do 'manners' come from?

6 Why do people say 'please'? Is it good to say 'please'? When? Why?

7 Why do they say 'thank you'? Is it good to say 'thank you'? When? Why?

8 What is courtesy? How do we show courtesy (eg at home, in school, at mealtimes, on the road, in writing)?

9 What different customs of courtesy are there in other cultures (eg in greeting people)?

10 When should you show courtesy to others? Do you? Why?

Further activities

• Hold a Courtesy Day (or Week). Can you be polite to everyone, all the time?

- Act out a dramatic situation showing the effects of politeness and rudeness.

- Discuss how courtesy is shown in your school, home or culture.

- Write an account of what you think good manners are.

- Find out how to say 'please' and 'thank you' in different languages.

Thought for the day

'Manners maketh man.'
(William of Wykeham's motto, 1324-1404)

'There is not a single outward mark of courtesy that does not have a deep moral basis.'
(Goethe, 1749-1832)

6 CURIOSITY

Note: Teachers may make an OHP.

Thinking about the drawing

Key question: What does the drawing mean?

1 What is happening in this picture?

2 Who do you think the people in the picture are?

3 Do you think they are boys or girls? Why?

4 What do you think the person on the left is feeling? What makes you think so?

5 Can you guess or tell what someone is feeling by looking at them? How?

6 What is the person on the right of the picture doing? How do you know?

7 What could he (or she) is feeling? What might he (or she) be saying?

8 Do you think they are friends? Could they not be friends? Why?

9 What might happen next?

10 What title could you give this picture?

Thinking about curiosity

Key question: What does being curious mean?

1 Are you a curious person?

2 What is curiosity?

3 Is curiosity a good thing? When is it right, or wrong, to be curious?

4 Curious people often ask questions. Is this a good thing? Why?

5 Are people born curious or do they become curious? If so, how?

6 Are all people curious? Give an example.

7 Should you be curious about other people? Why?

8 There is a saying: 'Curiosity killed the cat'. What does it mean?

9 What are you most curious about? What would you most like to know?

10 Do you ever wonder? What is 'wonder'?

Further activities

- Collect questions that people would most like to have answered.
- Survey children of different ages. Are they curious? What are they curious about?
- Invite an interesting local person to be interviewed, and to interview a child or group.
- Create a list of questions to send to, and find out about, a well-known person of your choice.
- Create a poem containing as many questions as you can.

Thought for the day

'One was presented with a small hairy individual and out of general curiosity, one climbed on.'
(Princess Anne, on her first encounter with a horse)

7 EMPATHY

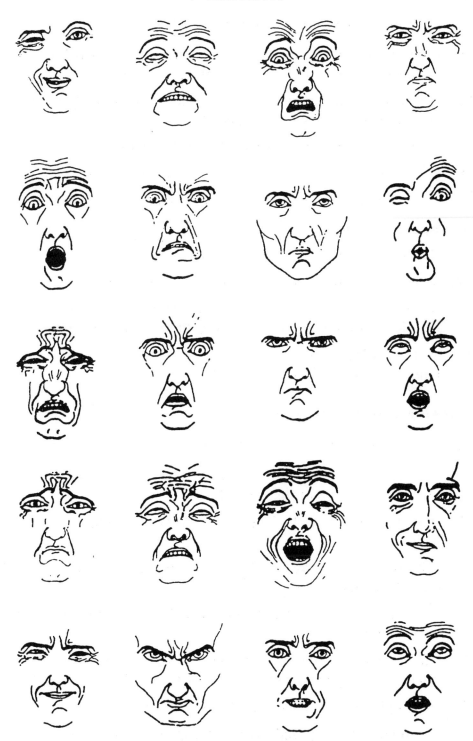

From *The Art of Pantomime* by John Aubrey, 1927

Note: Teachers may make an OHP.

Thinking about the illustrations

Key question: What do the illustrations show?

1   Look at each face. Do you think it shows a positive feeling, a negative feeling, neither, or more than one feeling?

2   How would you describe each face? Can you find a different word to describe each expression?

3   What is it in a face that shows the expression of feeling?

4   Which feature in each human face is most expressive?

5   Can you tell if the faces are male or female? Explain why.

6   Do you think each face is of the same person?

7   How old do you think the person (or people) shown might be?

8   Can a face express more than one emotion? Give an example.

9   Do you think the drawings illustrate *all* possible human emotions? What expressions or emotions are not illustrated?

10   With any of the faces can you suggest what might have happened to cause that expression?

Thinking about feelings and emotions

Key question: What are feelings and emotions?

1   What is a feeling or emotion? Can you have more than one feeling or emotion at the same time?

2   Why do people have feelings? Does everyone have the same feelings?

3   Is it possible to cause people to feel good or bad (happy or sad)? Give an example.

4   Can you make yourself feel good or bad (happy or sad)? Explain why or how.

5   Can you always tell how a person feels by the way they look? What other ways are there to express feelings?

6   Do people hide their feelings? When and why?

7   Is it good to show or hide your feelings? Give examples.

8   Are some people better at expressing their feelings than others? Why?

9 Do you always know how you are feeling, or how others are feeling? Why?

10 Is it possible to control your feelings? Give an example.

Further activities

- Collect pictures of human faces. Discuss what each may be feeling and why.

- Study masks from different cultures. Draw or create masks of faces that express different emotions.

- Choose an emotion as a topic for writing eg 'Anger is...', 'Fear is...', 'Sadness is...'

- Mime feelings or emotions for others to guess.

- Consider works of art eg a poem, picture or piece of music, and discuss the feelings that each expresses or arouses. Discuss whether words, colours or sounds express feelings.

Thought for the day

'O wad some Pow'r the giftie gie us/To see ousels as others see us!'

(*Robert Burns 1759–1796, from 'To a Louse'*)

8 FAIRNESS

The Troll's Share

There was once a farmer who was a very hard worker. He was most careful to get everything he possibly could out of his land. One year when he was sowing his crops he noticed a small hill in the middle of one of his fields. Nothing was growing on it but weeds and grass.

'That'll never do,' he said to himself. And at once he began to plough over the mound.

As he pulled the plough across the hill it suddenly began to shake. Then it rose like a mushroom, held up by four red pillars. The farmer knew at once that he had been trying to plough up the roof of a Troll's house. The Trolls were ugly monsters that hated the sunshine. They lived underground, but at night they raised the roofs of their houses on pillars and crawled out. The Troll who lived in this hill-house was sitting there, shaded by his earthy roof. He peered angrily at the farmer, and bellowed, 'Who has dared to plough up the roof of my house! How dare you meddle with us earth-dwellers!'

Trolls were fearsome creatures. The farmer, taking courage in his hands, crept up to the edge of the house, making sure he kept well out of reach of the Troll.

'I beg your pardon, Mister Troll,' said the farmer, as politely as he could. 'I had no idea that this hill was your roof. It was sitting here doing nothing and it seemed a pity to waste good ground.'

'Hmm,' grunted the Troll, 'and what are you going to do with it?'

'Why, plant crops on it,' said the farmer. 'I could grow plenty of good food up there on the roof of your house.'

'Well, it's my house,' grumbled the Troll, 'and the only person who should grow things on it is me.'

'You're quite right,' said the farmer. 'But it would mean a great deal of trouble for you, and hard work which I know you won't like. And there is the sunshine. I know that gentlemen like yourself who live underground hate to work in sunlight. Why not let me sow the crops for you and we can share whatever grows on your roof? One year I'll take the part that grows above ground, and you can have what grows under it. The next year I'll have what's under the soil and you can have what's above it.'

The Troll scratched one of his heads. He had three of them, but none had many brains inside.

'That seems fair,' he muttered. 'You seem a good strong fellow. All right, it's a deal. I shall have the first crop which grows above the ground, and you can have the roots. Next year I'll have the crops beneath the soil and you'll have what grows above it.'

The farmer promised that he would keep his side of the bargain. The Troll thanked him, his mouths began to yawn and he settled down to sleep again. Slowly his house sank under the ground until nothing showed but the little hill which was its roof. The farmer went on with his ploughing, smiling to himself at the thought of the bargain he had made with the ugly Troll.

After he had finished ploughing the farmer sowed carrots all over the hill. They grew well and at harvest time he gathered a heavy crop. According to the bargain the farmer kept the carrots themselves, since they grew underground, while the Troll had the useless tops. Next year the farmer sowed a fine field of wheat across the roof of the Troll's house. When it was ripe he harvested the crop for himself, according to the bargain, and dug up all the roots for the Troll.

So the farmer had a harvest of carrots and a harvest of corn in alternate years, and the Troll had his share of carrot tops and corn roots. The farmer was pleased, and the Troll was content, since he knew no better even though he had three heads.

(Danish folktale)

Thinking about the story

Key question: What does the story mean?

1   What sort of person was the farmer?

2   What is a Troll?

3   In what ways is the Troll like the farmer?

4   In what ways is the Troll different from the farmer?

5   What bargain did the farmer make with the Troll?

6   Was it a fair bargain?

7   Did the farmer keep his side of the bargain? How?

8   What would be good, bad or interesting about having three heads like the Troll?

9   Could Trolls exist? Do you think people believe in them? Why?

10   What do you think the moral of this story is?

Thinking about fairness

Key question: What is being fair?

1   What does it mean to be fair?

2   What should you be fair about? Give an example.

3   When is it hard to be fair?

4   What is fair play? Give examples of what is fair and not fair in games.

5   How can you make sure people are playing fairly?

6   What do you think is not fair in your life?

7   What is fair or not fair about your class/school?

8   What rules do you think would be fair in your class/school/home?

9   Are people fairly treated in life? Is anyone not treated fairly? Say why, or why not.

10   Is it a fair world? How could we make it a better or fairer world?

Further activities

• Discuss a problem in the news, and a fair way to solve the problem.

• Make up a game which is fair for all the players.

• Interview a referee or someone who has to ensure fair play.

• Write about what you think is unfair eg using the title: 'It's not fair!'

• Make a list of rules for your class, school, or home.

Thought for the day

'Everyone is entitled in full equality to a fair and public hearing.'*(Article 10, Universal Declaration of Human Rights)*

9 FORGIVENESS

The Bishop's Candlesticks

Many years ago there lived in the town of Dijon in France a kindly old bishop. He was generous to all in need, no beggar was ever turned away from his door, and no one who needed help was ever refused.

One day a poor traveller arrived in town. He was a large, rough-looking man in dirty ragged clothes. His face was sullen and he had a wild look in his eyes. People in the town were at once suspicious of this strange man and no innkeeper would give him a bed for the night. At last a woman took pity on the weary man and directed him to the bishop's house.

The bishop was sitting before a fire waiting for his evening meal. Suddenly the door burst open. It was the wild-looking stranger.

'I am looking for lodgings,' he said, 'and I was sent to your door. My name is Jean Valjean and I am a convict. I have been in prison for nineteen years. No one will give me a room for the night, not even a kennel to sleep in. I have walked all day and I can't go any further. Will you give me a little food and let me sleep in your stable?'

'Come in,' said the bishop. 'You are welcome. Warm yourself by the fire, have supper with me and stay the night.'

So the convict stayed, ate a meal with the bishop by candlelight and was given a clean bed to sleep in. After supper the bishop took one of the silver candlesticks that he had received as a Christmas present and showed Jean his room. But that night as he lay in bed, Jean Valjean did not think of the food that he had eaten; he was remembering the gleaming silver knives and forks he had used for supper, and made up his mind to steal them. When all was quiet, he crept downstairs, took all the silver he could find into his bag and escaped into the night.

When the bishop rose next morning he was surprised to see that his guest and his silver had gone. Soon there came a knock at the door and there between two policemen stood Jean Valjean.

'We caught him running away with a bag full of silver,' said the policeman.

'Oh, there you are,' said the bishop to Jean Valjean. 'I'm glad you came back. You forgot the candlesticks. I meant to give you those as well.' And he handed his silver candlesticks to Jean.

'So you gave him the silver?' said the policeman in surprise. 'We thought he was a thief.'

'I have given him the silver so that he can make a new start in his life,' said the bishop. 'Please let him go.'

The convict could hardly believe his ears, and tried to thank the bishop.

'Do not thank me,' said the bishop. 'Just remember you have promised to use the money to become an honest man.'

Jean Valjean did not remember having promised anything, but always remembered the bishop who had forgiven him, and he kept the bishop's candlesticks for the rest of his life.

(Adapted from Victor Hugo's 'Les Miserables')

Thinking about the story

Key question: What does the story mean?

1   What is a bishop? Where did the bishop live?

2   Who was Jean Valjean? What do we know of his life?

3   Why were the people suspicious of him? Were they right to be suspicious? Why?

4   Why did Jean go to the bishop's house?

5   Why at night did he lay in bed thinking of the bishop's knives and forks?

6   Why did the bishop offer the silver candlesticks to Jean?

7   What did the bishop say Jean had promised?

8   Why do you think Jean always remembered the bishop?

9   Do you think Jean changed after this experience? Why?

10   What other title might this story have?

Thinking about forgiveness

Key question: What does forgiveness mean?

1   When are people forgiven for what they have done wrong?

2   Why are people sometimes forgiven for doing wrong?

3   Do you find it easy or difficult to forgive other people? Why?

4   What do you do when you forgive someone? Give an example.

5   What do you feel when you forgive someone?

6   What do you do if you want to be forgiven for something you have done wrong?

7   Are there some things you would never forgive? If so, what and why?

8   Do you find it easy to forgive yourself? Why? Give an example.

9   Should everyone be given a second chance if they have done wrong? Why?

10   When is it good to 'forgive and forget'? Are there some things we should never forgive or forget?

Further activities

• Act and discuss a parable about forgiveness eg The Prodigal Son (Luke 15) or The Unmerciful Servant (Matthew 18).

• Write your own story about forgiveness (or the lack of it).

• Find out what a feud is. Write a report about a famous feud eg Romeo and Juliet.

• Think about something you have done wrong and wish to be forgiven for.

• Find out how to say sorry (or ask for pardon) in as many languages as you can.

Thought for the day

> 'To err is human, to forgive divine.'
>
> *(Alexander Pope, 1688-1744)*

10 FREEDOM

Diogenes and his Barrel

Over two thousand years ago there lived in Greece a rich man called Diogenes. He lived in a large house and had many servants to look after him. He owned vineyards and orchards. He had dancers and musicians, and singers to sing for him.

But none of this made Diogenes happy. He was always so busy seeing people and doing things. There was work on the farm to be done, and the house to clean. There were things to buy and things to sell. His servants would quarrel, and his fields would get flooded. He had plenty of money but people kept telling him what he should and what he shouldn't be doing with it. There seemed to be no end to his problems. Although he was rich he was not happy.

What Diogenes really liked doing was to walk in the forest – there he felt free. Perhaps he would sit under a tree and read, or just look at things for a long time and think about them. But even in the forest his happiness never lasted long, for his servants and advisers would follow him and pester him with their questions.

'Should we do this, or do that?' asked his advisers.

'Should we buy this or buy that?' asked his servants.

'Oh, fuss and bother,' grumbled Diogenes.

So one day Diogenes called all the servants of his household together. 'I am not happy,' he said. 'Everything I own gives me trouble. I want to live a simple life. I want to travel so that I can see things and talk to people.'

Diogenes had decided what he would do to be free. He gave a party for his friends and gave away everything that he owned, his house and his furniture, his fields and his farm, even his clothes. His friends were pleased, but his servants were worried. 'What will become of us?' they cried.

'Men should not be slaves,' Diogenes told them. 'You are all free to go.'

'But how will we live?' asked his servants.

'You must find your own way,' said Diogenes.

'But how will you live,' they asked, 'now that you have given everything away?'

Diogenes pointed to his dog, 'I will live a simple life as he does,' said Diogenes. 'He is happy yet he does not own a thing.'

Taking with him only his drinking cup Diogenes set off. There was a ship in the harbour, and he decided to go wherever it took him.

'From now on,' said Diogenes, 'I am a citizen of the world.'

Eventually Diogenes arrived at Athens, the capital of Greece, and there by a well he saw a young boy drinking water with cupped hands. Diogenes looked at the only thing he carried. 'Why, I don't even need my drinking cup,' he said, and threw it away. Now he had nothing.

Diogenes had nowhere to sleep, but he found an old barrel that nobody wanted and he made it his home. People came from far and wide to see the strange sight of Diogenes living in his barrel. He loved to sit in the sun and talk to the people who came to see him. Soon he had many friends and he became famous for his wise words.

'You don't have to own anything to be happy,' he would tell them. Some people in Athens offered Diogenes a fine house to live in, but he replied, 'No thank you, I'd rather stay here in my barrel.'

One day the king, Alexander the Great, returned from his long travels. His army had won many battles. He had conquered a great empire that stretched from Greece to India. He thought nothing more important than his power and his possessions. When he was told about Diogenes giving all his possessions away and being happy living in a barrel he wanted to meet him.

So the mighty Alexander went to see Diogenes, and found him lying outside his barrel, fast asleep. 'Wake up, Diogenes!' ordered the king. Diogenes opened one eye and then shut it again.

'I can give you anything in the world,' said the king. 'Tell me what you want and you shall have it.'

'I want you to step aside,' said Diogenes. 'You're blocking out the sun.'

'Is that all?' asked Alexander. Diogenes smiled and nodded. Without another word Alexander walked away. The sun shone down on the face of Diogenes. He had found a place where he could sit and think, without fuss or bother, and where life was simple and he was free – living in a barrel.

(Greek legend)

Thinking about the story

Key question: What does the story mean?

1   At the start of the story, was Diogenes rich or poor? How do we know?

2   Was he happy or unhappy? Why was this?

3   What did Diogenes really like doing? Why?

4   How did he feel about his life? Why?

5   What did Diogenes decide to do? Why?

6   Who was Alexander the Great?

7   Why did Alexander want to meet Diogenes?

8   What happened when Alexander went to meet Diogenes?

9   Diogenes was famous for his wise words. What does this mean?

10   Could the story have been true? Why?

Thinking about freedom

Key question: What does it mean to be free?

1   Diogenes felt free when he was walking in the forest. When do you feel free?

2   What does it mean to feel free?

3   Is feeling free the same as being free?

4   What are you free to do?

5   What are you not free to do?

6   Could anyone be perfectly free? What would this mean?

7   What is the opposite of being free?

8 Do you live in a free country? What does this mean?

9 What does it mean not to be free?

10 Is freedom a good thing? Why?

Further activities

- Draw a cartoon version of Diogenes and his barrel.

- Imagine you are a slave. Write about your life and feelings.

- Find out why in the USA they have Independence Day and the Statue of Liberty.

- Hold a free debate, vote or referendum on a controversial issue.

- Find and discuss a news item about people who are struggling for freedom.

Thought for the day:

> 'A world founded on four essential freedoms. First is freedom of speech and expression – everwhere in the world. The second is freedom of every person to worship God in his own way – everywhere in the world. The third is freedom from want ... everywhere in the world. The fourth is freedom from fear ... anywhere in the world.'
>
> *(Franklin D. Roosevelt, 1941)*

11 FRIENDSHIP

Best Friends

Would a best friend
Eat your last sweet
Talk behind your back
Have a party and not ask you?

Mine did.

Would your best friend
Borrow your bike without telling you
Deliberately forget your birthday
Avoid you whenever possible?

Mine did.

Would your best friend
Turn up on your bike
Give you a whole packet of your favourite sweets
Look you in the eye?

Mine did.

Would your best friend say
Sorry I talked about you behind your back
Sorry I had a party and didn't invite you
Sorry I deliberately forgot your birthday
– I thought you'd fallen out with me

Mine did.

And would a best friend say
Never mind
That's OK.

I did.

Bernard Young

Thinking about the poem

Key question: What does the poem mean?

 1   The poem is called Best Friends. Who are 'best friends'?

 2   Would a best friend eat your last sweet? Why?

 3   Would a best friend talk about you behind your back? Why?

 4   Would a best friend have a party and not ask you? Why?

 5   Would a best friend borrow your bike without telling you? Why might this happen?

 6   Would a best friend deliberately forget your birthday or avoid you whenever possible?

 7   Why do you think the poet's best friend did these things?

 8   Have your best friends ever done these or similar things to you?

 9   Why might the best friend think the poet had 'fallen out' with him?

10   Why do you think the poet said 'Never mind/That's OK'?

Thinking about friends

Key question: What is a friend?

 1   How many friends have you got, do you think?

 2   If someone is your friend, must they also think you are their friend?

 3   Can you be a friend of somebody you don't like?

 4   If somebody doesn't like you, can you still be their friend?

 5   Do you have a best friend? What makes them a best friend?

 6   Are you the best friend of somebody? How do you know?

 7   What is the difference between a friend and a best friend?

 8   Could you live without any friends? What would that be like?

 9   How do you make a friend? How do you become a best friend?

10   Have you ever forgiven a friend? Has a friend ever forgiven you? Give an example.

Further activities

- Write a list of characteristics of a best friend eg 'A best friend is someone who ...'

- Write a poem, story or description of forgiving a friend for what they have said or done.

- Describe your best friend, without saying who they are.

- Listen to Elgar's *Enigma Variations*. Choose or play music to describe a friend.

- Make up a play about a quarrel between friends. Show how the quarrel is resolved.

Thought for the day

'A friend in need is a friend indeed.'

(English proverb)

12 GENEROSITY

The Gift of Camels

The Arabs have always been great mathematicians. The numbers that we use were originally Arabic numbers. Here is an Arab story in which there is some mathematics. But what is worth thinking about in the story is not just the mathematics. Here is the story.

One day an old Arab sheikh died. Although he was the chief of his tribe he was not a rich man. All his wealth lay in his 'ships of the desert', the camels that he owned. His camels had provided him with food and milk, with transport across the sandy wastes, and with skins to make his tents. He had three sons, and now that he had died they would own his camels. But first they would have to listen to the reading of the old man's will, to see how the old man had decided to share his camels out between them.

The whole family gathered together in the old man's tent. His three sons were there ready to hear their uncle read the old man's will. The uncle read out how the herd of camels were to be divided between the three sons. The eldest would receive half the camels, the second would receive one third of them, and the youngest would receive one ninth. The will ended with these words: 'Whatever you give in love, it shall come back to you.'

The sons had now been told how their father wanted the camels shared between them, but they were not sure how many camels the old man had. So they quickly rounded up the whole herd, and counted them. There were seventeen camels. What did the will say about how they were to be divided? The eldest was to receive half of them, but what was half of seventeen? The next was to receive a third, but what was a third of seventeen? The youngest was to receive one ninth, but what was one ninth of seventeen? Try as they might the three brothers could not work out how many each should have. So they asked the best mathematicians in the tribe. But none could solve the problem. What were they to do?

They decided to go to their uncle, to see if he could help. The uncle thought he would check the will and read it again ... ending with the words: 'Whatever you give in love, it shall come back to you.' What did those words mean? He thought long and hard. Finally a smile spread across his face.

'Now I understand what I must do,' he said. 'I will give you one of my camels to add to the others. That will solve the problem.' The brothers looked bewildered and scratched their heads. How would being given another camel help? Of course! Now there would be eighteen camels. The oldest son quickly thought of his share, and worked out what half of eighteen was. The next son thought of his share, and worked out a third of eighteen. The youngest thought of his share, and worked out one ninth of eighteen. The camels could now be divided according to the father's will. Of eighteen camels the oldest would have nine, the next one six and the youngest two. How many camels was that? Seventeen! There was one camel over. What on earth would they do with the extra camel?

The three sons soon agreed on what they should do. They thought it would only be right to give their uncle his camel back. The old uncle was pleased, but not at all surprised.

'I knew something would come back to me,' he said. 'Whatever you give in love, will one day come back to you.'

(Arab story)

Thinking about the story

Key question: what does the story mean?

1   The story is about an old Arab sheikh and his family. What do we know about the sheikh?

2   What do we not know about the sheikh?

3   Why were camels so important to the sheikh?

4   What is a will? What did the old man's will say?

5   Why did the three boys go to see their uncle?

6   How did the uncle solve the problem?

7   Why did the uncle say: 'I knew something would come back to me'?

8   Do you think there is a message or moral in this story?

9   What does the last line: 'Whatever you give in love, will one day come back to you' mean?

10 Do you think it is true? Always, sometimes or never? Why?

Thinking about generosity

Key question: What is generosity?

1 What is a gift?

2 What special times are there for giving and receiving presents?

3 Why do we give presents at these times? Do we give gifts at other times? Why?

4 Which is more important, the gift or the thought behind the giving? Why?

5 Are there some things that are given that cannot be touched or seen?

6 Some say we are given gifts from God or nature. What gifts do they mean?

7 If someone gives you a gift how should you respond?

8 What is the best gift you have ever been given?

9 Is it good to be generous? Why? Give an example.

10 Is it better to give or to receive? Why?

Further activities

• Make up your own version of the story, using the same way of dividing the numbers.

• Retell the story in picture form to present to younger children.

• Make a display of gifts the children would like to give, to whom and why eg Mum – an extra day at the weekend!

• Make a list of the gifts you would like to receive. (Think of some gifts that don't cost any money!)

• Make small gifts to give to younger children, friends or those in need.

Thought for the day

> 'It is more blessed to give than to receive.'
> *(The Bible, Acts of the Apostles 20:35)*

12 GREED

The Pardoner's Tale

There were three men who sat drinking in a tavern early one morning. And as they sat they heard a bell ringing outside. One of the men called the boy of the house to go and see why the bell was ringing. The boy was soon back with the answer.

'Sir,' said the boy, 'it is a funeral going by. A friend of yours, sir, has been killed by a secret thief that men call Death. Death has killed many people in this land. He is our great enemy. Be prepared to meet him at any time. That is what my mother taught me.'

'By Saint Mary,' said the innkeeeper, 'the boy speaks true. This year Death has killed man, woman and child, servant and page in a village only a mile away. I think he lives there, but it's as well to keep out of his way if you can.'

'Why?' said one of the drinkers. 'Is it so dangerous to meet him? Let us go and search for him, my friends. Let's kill this treacherous villain called Death.'

The three men swore an oath that they would be as brothers, ready to live and die for each other. Without delay they set off for the village of which the innkeeper had spoken. They were determined that Death would die, if they could catch him.

They had gone nearly half a mile and were about to cross a stile when they met a poor old man. The old man was completely wrapped in black, except for his face.

'How now, old man,' said the first drinker. 'Perhaps you can help us. We are looking for Death. We have heard that he lives somewhere in these parts, and we mean to find him.'

'God bless you, sirs,' said the strange old man. 'I know the very place that you will find him.'

'Where, where?' said each of the men.

'You will find him in that field yonder,' said the black figure, pointing his finger.

The three men went straight to the field and there under an oak tree they saw something which amazed them. A huge pile of coins lay there waiting for them. The coins were gold and they glittered in the sunshine.

'We're rich, we're rich!' cried one of the men.

'Wait a minute,' said another, 'we'd better not let anyone else see this. Let's wait until nightfall and carry it home when no one else can see us.'

They all agreed that this was a good idea. While they waited they sent the youngest man back to the village to buy some food to eat and wine to drink. The young man set off for the village.

When he was gone the two men who had stayed to guard the treasure began plotting. Which would be more, a third share – or a half? They soon agreed that when the young man returned they would kill him and take his share of the treasure for themselves. 'It'll be easy,' they thought, 'there are two of us and only one of him.'

It so happened that as the young man walked to the village a wicked idea came into his mind. He went to an apothecary's shop (a kind of chemist) and said he wanted to kill some rats. Back he went with two bottles of poison and a bottle of wine for himself.

As soon as the young man got back the other two leapt on him and stabbed him to death. The two murderers felt very pleased with themselves and turned their greedy eyes on the piles of gold.

'Let us drink and make merry,' said one, 'before we share out treasure.' He picked up one of the bottles, took a long swig and handed it to the other man who also drank deeply. It was a bottle of poison. Within seconds the murderers fell upon their gold ... dead.

The greedy men had found what they were looking for.

(*A story from* The Canterbury Tales *by Geoffrey Chaucer, 1340-1400*)

Thinking about the story

Key question: What does the story mean?

1   What bell was ringing? Why was the bell ringing?
2   Why did the innkeeper think Death lived in the next village?
3   What did the drinkers decide to try to find and do?

4   What oath did they swear? What is an oath?

5   Whom did they meet on the way?

6   What did the men find in the field?

7   Why did they decide to wait until nightfall?

8   What did the men plan? Did their plans work?

9   Why did the men die?

10 The story says they 'found what they were looking for'. Do you agree?

Thinking about greed and self control

Key question: What do greed and self control mean?

1   What is a greedy person?

2   Do you ever feel greedy? When? Why?

3   People sometimes feel greedy for things other than food. What are people greedy for?

4   Not everyone is greedy. Do you know someone who is not greedy? Why are they not greedy?

5   Is it a good thing to feel greedy? Is it a good thing to be greedy? Why?

6   Can you help feeling greedy? Can you stop yourself from feeling greedy? How, or why?

7   Is greed dangerous? Give an example.

8   Are animals greedy? Is there a difference between human and animal greed?

9   Do you find it easy to control yourself? When is it easy? When is it hard?

10 Is being able to control yourself a good thing? Why?

Further activities

•   Use drama or mime to enact your own version of the story.

•   List the things people feel most greedy about, and arrange them in order of importance.

- Read a fable by Aesop about greed. Write your own fable about the consequences of greed.

- Investigate a range of advertisements. Which advertisements promote greed?

- Study the topic of conservation. Discuss ways of conserving the world's finite resources.

Thought for the day

> 'Suppose everybody cared enough, everybody shared enough, wouldn't everybody have enough? There is enough in the world for everyone's need but not for everyone's greed.'
>
> *(Frank Buchman 1878-1961)*

14 HELPING OTHERS

The Green Bottle

There was once a King who owned a very special green bottle. Inside the bottle was a liquid which was believed to be the elixir of life, something that would cure any disease, that would bring life to a dying man, that could help the person who drank it to live forever. After centuries of searching for something that could be eaten or drunk to give everlasting life, someone had at last succeeded. A small amount of this precious liquid was kept inside the green bottle.

One day the King was told that a prisoner in the palace jail was very ill. Years ago the poor man had stolen some food, and now it was only a short while before he was due to be released. But the old man was ill and afraid that he would die before seeing the wonders of the outside world once more. So he sent a message to the King begging for a drop of the elixir so that he would live long enough to see his family and friends again.

The King refused, saying that he was keeping it for someone who really needed it. Soon afterwards the poor prisoner died.

Some time later a young man was badly injured in an accident, and his crippled mother went to the King asking for a drop of the precious elixir to save her son. If he died she would have no-one to look after her.

The King considered her case carefully, but said no, he would keep it for someone who really deserved it. Not long after that the old woman's son died.

As time went by many sick and dying people begged the King for a drop of the elixir from his green bottle, but always the answer was the same. The King was keeping it for someone who really needed it. Gradually people came to suspect that the King was saving the elixir for no-one but himself.

Then one day the King became ill. The doctors tried every possible cure but nothing seemed to help. Each day the King grew worse. As time went by he became convinced that he was dying. Only one thing, he thought, could save him. He sent for his most trusted servant to tell him the secret place where the elixir was kept.

'Bring me the green bottle,' he gasped.

The servant went at once, found the green bottle and handed it over to his royal master. The King took it in his trembling hands. Slowly and carefully he removed the cork and brought the bottle to his open lips.

The King tried to drink, but to his horror he found there was nothing there. The bottle was empty! There was not a drop of the elixir left. How could that be? The King again put the bottle to his lips but nothing came out. There was nothing to drink. The bottle was empty. He had kept it locked away for all those years. He had hoped it would help him live forever. Now all he had were regrets – and an empty green bottle.

(Italian legend)

Note. In the cathedral of Genoa in Italy there is a green bottle which is said to be the legendary bottle which once contained the elixir of life.

Thinking about the story

Key question: what does the story mean?

1   What is an elixir of life? What kind of liquid might it have been?

2   Why did the King want the elixir?

3   Who begged the King for a drop of the elixir? Were they given any? Why?

4   Whom was the King keeping the elixir for?

5   Where do you think the King might have kept the green bottle?

6   What happened when the King went to drink the elixir? Why did he want to drink it?

7   What might have happened to the liquid in the green bottle?

8   Why did the King have regrets? What do you think his regrets were?

9   What do you think happened to the King, and to the bottle?

10   Do you think there is a moral to this story? If so, what is the moral?

Thinking about helping others

Key question: Why should we help others?

1   What does being selfish mean? Give an example.

2   Are we all selfish at times?

3   What would the world be like if everyone was selfish all the time?

4   Do we need to help others in life? Why?

5   Do we need other people to help us? When?

6   Which people are particularly in need of help? How should they be helped?

7   Does everyone need help at some time?

8   Is it important to help other people? Why?

9   Who spends their lives helping others? Why do people help others?

10 How could you, or I, help others more?

Further activities

• Write a story about, or design an advertisement for, a potion to help to solve a human problem.

• Not all liquids are safe to drink. List as many as you can that are dangerous to drink.

• Discuss reasons for and against living forever.

• Choose a charity for helping others and discuss ways of raising money for it.

• Interview someone whose work involves helping others.

Thought for the day

> 'I get by with a little help from my friends.'
> *(Song by John Lennon and Paul McCartney)*

15 IDEALS

Imagine

Imagine there's no heaven,
It's easy if you try,
No hell below us,
Above us only sky,
5 Imagine all the people
Living for today ...

Imagine there's no countries,
It isn't hard to do,
Nothing to kill or die for,
10 No religion too,
Imagine all the people
Living life in peace.

Imagine no possessions,
I wonder if you can,
15 No need for greed or hunger
A brotherhood of man,
Imagine all the people
Sharing all the World.

You may say I'm a dreamer,
20 But I'm not the only one,
I hope some day you'll join us,
And the world will live as one.

John Lennon

Thinking about the song

Key question: What does the song mean?

1   What does it mean to imagine something?

2   What is 'heaven' (line 1) and 'hell' (line 3)?

3   Do you agree that imagining 'is easy if you try'(line 2)?

4   What does 'all the people living for today' (lines 5/6) mean?

5   Can you 'imagine there's no countries' (line 7)? Could our world exist without countries?

6   What do people 'kill or die for' (line 9)?

7   Could we live without 'religion' (line 10)?

8   Can you imagine living 'with no possessions' (line 13)?

9   What does 'a brotherhood of man' (line 16) mean?

10   Why do you think John Lennon wrote this song? What is a dreamer? Are you a 'dreamer'?

Thinking about ideals

Key question: What are ideals?

1   When you have a 'dream' does it mean you are dreaming?

2   Can you imagine an ideal world? What is an ideal world?

3   What would your ideal world be like?

4   Could there ever be an ideal world?

5   What would help create an ideal world?

6   What would your ideal person be like?

7   Is there, or has there ever been, an ideal person?

8   What sort of person do you want to be?

9   What would help you become the sort of person you would like to be?

10   What is an 'ideal'? Is an ideal always imaginary or can it be real?

Further activities

- Draw a picture of your ideal world, or ideal person.

- Find the words of other lyrics by John Lennon. Discuss why you do or do not like the words of a particular song.

- Create a picture, frieze or collage symbolising the brotherhood of man.

- Listen to the song 'Imagine' by John Lennon. Create a dance/movement expressing the words and music.

- Write your own poem, song or story with the title 'Imagine'.

Thought for the day

'Imagination grows by exercise.'

(Somerset Maugham 1874-1965)

16 JUSTICE

The Justice of Dick Whittington

Before there was TV, radio, or newspapers, the news of the day was brought by town criers who walked the city streets each day ringing a bell and then calling out the news.

One day a town crier walked through the city of London shouting, 'Oyea! Oyea! Oyea! A bag of 200 gold coins has been lost. A reward of half this money is offered to anyone who finds it!'

All who heard the town crier kept a special lookout for the lost bag. It so happened that a poor young sailor who was drinking in a tavern found a bag lying under his bench. To his amazement he found the bag was full of coins – gold coins. Thoughts raced through his mind. What should he do? Though he was poor, he was honest. He hurried out of the tavern, and ran after the town crier to tell him that the bag had been found.

'You're lucky!' said the town crier. 'The man who lost the bag is a merchant named Andreas. He's staying at the Tabard Inn in Southwark. Take it to him and you'll get a reward.'

The young sailor took the bag with him to the inn where the rich merchant was staying. The merchant was overjoyed to get his bag of gold back. He poured coins out onto the table, and slowly counted them.

'I suppose you'll be wanting your reward?' the merchant asked the sailor.

'If you please, sir,' said the sailor. 'My mother is a widow and we are very poor. With a little money I can give her a home and perhaps start myself up in a trade.'

But as the merchant counted his coins, other thoughts began to enter his head. Now the money was safe, how could he avoid giving the sailor his reward? He had an idea.

'You thief!' he cried. 'Where's my diamond? My diamond was worth ten bags of gold. It was here in my purse with the coins. Now it has gone. What have you done with it?'

The poor sailor did not know what to say. 'There was no jewel there,' he replied. 'I am no thief.'

'Either you give me back the diamond and take your reward, or begone from here, you thief!'

The sailor felt angry at being called a thief. 'We shall see who is the thief!' he cried. 'Come with me to the Lord Mayor. He shall judge my case. Although I am a poor man he will treat me fairly.'

'Huh! He'll put you in jail more likely,' sneered the merchant. So off they went to the court.

At this time the Lord Mayor was Dick Whittington, the most famous Lord Mayor of London. When their turn came, first the merchant, then the sailor, told their stories. Dick Whittington listened carefully, and looked closely at the two men.

'Why,' he asked the merchant, 'did you not tell the town crier that the bag also contained a valuable diamond?'

'Ah,' said the crafty merchant, 'it was to test the honesty of the finder, my Lord.'

'Do you swear that the bag you lost contained 200 gold coins and a diamond?' asked the Mayor.

'I do,' said the merchant.

'And do you swear that the bag you found held only 200 pieces of gold?' he asked the sailor.

'I do,' he replied.

'Then the problem is solved,' said the Mayor. 'This cannot be the merchant's purse since there is no diamond in it. So it must belong to someone else. If that person does not claim it within forty days, the bag and the money belong to the sailor!'

The merchant's face turned very white. His mouth dropped open but no sound came out.

'I do hope,' said the Mayor, 'that someone will find your bag with the diamond in it.'

(English legend)

Thinking about the story

Key question: What does the story mean?

1   Before there was TV, radio, or newspapers how did people in cities hear the news?

2   What news did the town crier call out? Who heard the town crier?

3   What was lost? Who found it? Where was it found?

4   What thoughts raced through the sailor's mind, do you think, when he found the bag?

5   What did he decide to do? Why?

6   How did the merchant respond when the sailor brought him his bag?

7   What reward did the sailor expect to get? Did he get it? Why?

8   Why did they go to the Lord Mayor? What is a Lord Mayor? Who was the Lord Mayor?

9   How did the Lord Mayor solve the dispute?

10 Do you think the Lord Mayor's action was just? Why?

Thinking about justice

Key question: What is justice?

1   When people say they want justice, what do they want?

2   Is justice the same as being fair? How do you treat people fairly (or with justice)?

3   What is the opposite of justice? What is injustice? Can you give an example?

4   What is a law court? What happens in a law court?

5   The symbol for justice on London's court of law (the Old Bailey) is a person holding a pair of scales. Why do you think a pair of scales is a symbol for justice?

6   The person holding the scales is also blindfolded. What do you think this represents?

7   In this country, people are said to be 'equal before the law'. What does this mean?

8   Courts of law protect human rights. What is a right? What does everyone have a right to?

9   Is life always always just and fair? Have you ever been unfairly treated?

10   Should you try to stop people being unfairly treated? Why? Give an example of this.

Further activities

* Interview someone whose job it is to ensure justice eg police officer, lawyer, judge.

* Display or draw a picture of the symbol of justice on top of the Old Bailey.

* Enact a court of law with defence, prosecution, accused, judge and jury.

* Debate a current problem of justice eg what should happen to robbers, murderers, asylum-seekers.

* Write and discuss something you think is unfair in life, under the title 'It's not fair!'

Thought for the day

'Whatsoever things are true, whatsoever things are honest, whatsoever things are just, whatsoever things are pure, whatsoever things are lovely, whatsoever things are of good report; if there be any virtue, if there be any praise, think on these things.'

(The Bible, Philippians 4:8)

17 LOVE

The Tiger's Whisker

Once a young woman named Yun Ok had a problem. So she went to the house of a mountain hermit to get help. The hermit was a famous wise man, who made lucky charms and magic potions.

'Why are you here?' asked the man.

'Oh famous wise man,' said Yun Ok, 'I am very miserable and worried. Make me a potion to solve my problem.'

'Everyone needs potions. We all think we can solve all our problems with a potion. Well, what is your story?'

'It is my husband,' said Yun Ok. 'I love him very much. He has been away for three years fighting in the wars. Now he has returned, he hardly speaks to me. When I speak, he doesn't seem to hear. When he talks, he speaks roughly to me. If I serve him food he doesn't like, he pushes it away and leaves the room. When he should be working in the rice field, I find him sitting on a hill staring out to sea.'

'That sometimes happens when young men come back from wars,' said the hermit.

'I want a potion, oh Wise One, to make my husband loving and gentle, as he used to be,' pleaded Yun Ok.

'Come back in three days,' said the hermit, 'and I will tell you what we need for the potion.'

Three days later Yun Ok returned to the hermit's house. The wise man told her that the most important ingredient he needed for the potion was a whisker from a living tiger.

'How can I possibly get that?' asked Yun Ok.

'If the potion is important enough,' said the hermit, 'you will succeed.'

Yun Ok went home and thought how she might get the tiger's whisker. Then one night while her husband was asleep, she crept out and went to the mountainside where the tiger lived. She had a bowl of rice and meat in her hand and held it out, calling for the tiger to come and eat. But the tiger did not come.

The next night Yun Ok went again, this time a little closer. Again she offered the bowl of food, but the tiger did not come. Every night she returned and each time moved closer to the tiger's cave. The tiger saw her but did not move.

One night Yun Ok came very close to the tiger's cave. This time the tiger came a few steps towards her and stopped. The two stood there looking at each other in the moonlight. The next night the same thing happened. The tiger came closer, and Yun Ok spoke to it in a soft voice. The following night the tiger ate the food she held out for him. And so for several nights the tiger ate, and Yun Ok gently rubbed its head with her hand.

Nearly six months after her first visit Yun Ok patted the animal and said, 'Oh Tiger, I must have one of your whiskers. Don't be angry!' And carefully she cut off one of his whiskers.

The tiger was not angry, and the next day Yun Ok took the tiger's whisker to the wise man.

The hermit studied the whisker. Satisfied it had come from the tiger, he then dropped it into his blazing fire.

'What have you done!' cried the woman.

'First tell me how you got it,' said the old man.

The woman told how she went to the mountain with a bowl of food, how she had spoken kindly to the tiger to win his confidence, how she had been patient and returned each night, how she had rubbed his head, and how only after he had made happy sounds had she asked him for his whisker.

'You tamed the tiger and won his confidence and love,' said the hermit.

'But I did it for nothing!' said Yun Ok. 'You have thrown the whisker into the fire!'

'No, it was not for nothing,' said the old man. 'The whisker is no longer needed. Is your husband more vicious than a tiger? Will he respond less to kindness and understanding? If you can tame a wild animal through love and kindness you can surely do the same with your husband.'

Yun Ok stood for a moment without saying a word. She then made her way home thinking about what she had learned from the wise man and the tiger.

(Folktale from Korea)

Thinking about the story

Key question: what does the story mean?

1 What was Yun Ok's problem?

2 Whom did she go to see? Why?

3 The old hermit was supposed to be wise. What does 'wise' mean?

4 Do you think someone is born wise or do they become wise? Why is that?

5 What is a potion? Could there be a 'magic potion'? Explain why.

6 Why might Yun Ok's husband behave as he did?

7 How did Yun Ok get the tiger's whisker?

8 What happened to the whisker? What did Yun Ok think would happen?

9 Why did the old hermit think the whisker was not needed?

10 What do you think Yun Ok had learnt from the Wise man and the tiger?

Thinking about love

Key question: What is love?

1 What does 'love' mean?

2 Is there a difference between real love and pretend love? Can you give an example?

3 Do we all need love? Why?

4 Whom do you love? Who do you think loves you? Can you choose who you love?

5 Is it possible to love everybody? Why?

6 Is it possible to love someone all the time?

7 Is loving someone the same as caring for them?

8 Can someone love you and hurt you at the same time?

9 How do you show someone you love them?

10 What is the difference between loving someone and liking them?

Further activities

- Think of a plan that you could use to get a tiger's whisker.

- Read and present a famous love story such as Shakespeare's *Romeo and Juliet*.

- Discuss in a Community of Enquiry the words of a recent pop song about love.

- Study the betrothal and marriage customs in different cultures.

- Write a list, poem or song starting 'Love is ...'

Thought for the day

'Thou shalt love thy neighbour as thyself.'
(The Bible, Matthew 19:19)

18 LOYALTY

When Did You Last See Your Father?

This is a story which is shown in a famous painting. It is said to have happened during the Civil War in England between the Cavaliers and the Roundheads.

The Cavaliers were royalists who fought on the side of King Charles 1 against the Roundheads who supported Parliament under their leader Oliver Cromwell. One of the officers in the Royalist army was Colonel Sydney. He had a daughter and a son who both dearly loved their Cavalier father. The Roundhead army were winning the war, and they were out to capture or kill all the Cavaliers they could find. Colonel Sydney knew that unless he hid he too would be captured by the Roundheads.

The family knew that the Roundhead army might arrive at any time to search for Cavaliers, so Colonel Sydney decided he had better hide in a small secret room in the house. His wife made the children promise not to say anything about where their father was hidden.

Soon after, just as they feared, there was a loud banging on the door. It was the Roundhead soldiers. They said they had come to find and arrest Colonel Sydney. They soldiers looked all over the house but could not find him and soon gave up the search. The family knew that very soon they might have some questions to answer.

First they questioned the boy's mother, then his older sister. They said they had not seen Colonel Sydney and did not know where he was. Now it was the turn of the young boy. The chief officer sat behind a big table. In the room were soldiers armed with swords and spears. The boy stood before them. He looked calm, but inside his heart was pounding and his hands trembled with fear. The soldiers had searched for his father and not found him. Now they waited to see what the boy would tell them.

'Now listen to me,' said the Chief, leaning forwards towards the boy. 'I am going to ask you a question. In the name of God do you promise to tell the truth?'

'Y – yes sir,' stammered the boy. Behind him he could hear that his sister was crying. His mother stood at the back of the room, looking worried.

'And when did you last see your father?' asked the Chief.

The boy paused. 'I saw him last night,' he answered.

'Last night, eh?' said the Chief. 'So he was here in the house last night?'

'Yes, sir.'

'And where in the house was he?'

'In my room,' said the boy.

'So your father came to see you last night?'

'Yes.'

'And where did he go after seeing you?'

'I don't know,' said the boy. 'I was asleep when he came, and asleep when he left.'

'What do you mean by that?'

'The last time I saw my father was in a dream.'

(This story is based on the picture 'And when did you last see your father?' by William Yeames (1835-1918), painted in 1878, which can be seen in the Walker Art Gallery in Liverpool.)

Thinking about the story

Key question: What does the story mean?

1   What is a civil war?

2   Who were the Roundheads and Cavaliers?

3   What do we know of the Sydney family?

4   Why did the Roundheads come to their house?

5   Why did they question the family?

6   What do you think the boy was feeling? What was he thinking?

7   What did the boy say? Did he tell the truth?

8   Where was the boy's father? Why was he not found?

9   Do you think the story is fact or fiction? Why?

10   What do you think happened next? How might the story end?

Thinking about loyalty

Key question: What does being loyal mean?

1   What does it mean to be loyal?

2   Is it important to be loyal to your friends? Why?

3   Do you expect your friends to be loyal to you? How would they show loyalty?

4   Should friends always be loyal? Would loyalty ever be wrong?

5   Can you think of a situation when you would expect your friends to be loyal?

6   Can you think of a time when you have been loyal to someone?

7   Who do you feel loyalty to? Why?

8   What does it mean to be loyal to your country? How do you show it?

9   What animals show loyalty? What do they do to be loyal?

10   The opposite of loyal is disloyal. What does this mean? Give an example.

Further activities

• Study a picture of the painting 'And when did you last see your father?' by the Victorian artist W. F. Yeames. Write your own version of the story.

• Act out the story in your own words, and create your own ending to the story.

• Discuss a dilemma about friendship: for example, if you see a friend steal from a shop what should you do?

• Research the events of the English Civil War. Find out about Oliver Cromwell.

• Discuss another story about loyalty eg 'The Bear that Spoke' (*Stories for Thinking* p 50)

Thought for the day

'It is better to be deceived by one's friends than to deceive them.'

(Goethe, 1749-1832)

19 MODESTY AND PRIDE

The Tinkling Medals

There was once in Russia a girl who was always winning prizes at school. The prizes that she won were little silver medals which she pinned to the front of her dress. Some prizes were for good behaviour, others were for working hard. She was very proud of all the medals she had won, and never stopped telling others how clever she was.

'Look at my medals,' she would say. 'No one has got as many medals as I have.' This was true. But nobody liked her for boasting about it. When other children won medals they took them home, but this girl would always wear hers, so that everyone could see how clever she was.

One day the headteacher announced that a wolf had been seen wandering around the wood near the school. It was winter and the wolf was probably feeling hungry.

'It has come to the village looking for food,' said the headteacher. 'You must be very careful when you go home. Always walk with some of your friends. You must not go home alone.'

When school was finished for the day everyone went home with their friends. Everyone, that is, except the girl with the medals. She was so bossy that she had no friends. She wasn't going to ask anyone to walk home with her. They could if they wanted. But none of them wanted to. So she set off alone on the path through the woods back to her home.

As she walked along she felt a little lonely. It was beginning to grow dark, and the wind whistled through the trees. But she could hear the medals chinking on her chest, and she knew that no one was as clever as she was.

Suddenly she saw a grey shadow in the trees. It disappeared, and then she saw it again. It was the wolf! She stopped and looked around. There was no one to be seen. Then she began walking quickly. She glanced back. The shadow was following her.

'I'd better hide,' she thought. So she ran through the trees as fast as her legs would carry her. Her heart was pounding. She saw a large bush and crouched quickly behind it. The leaves covered her completely. Here she would be safe.

The shadow of the wolf moved past where she was hiding, then it stopped. The wolf's ears pricked up, listening. The girl lay quite still in the bushes. She did not make a movement or a sound, but as she breathed the medals on her chest began to tinkle. The wolf had heard the faint sound of tinkling medals.

Although they searched the whole forest, the girl was never seen again. All that was found, beneath an old hedge, was a little heap of shining medals.

(Adapted from a story by Saki, H.H. Munro)

Thinking about the story

Key question: What does the story mean?

1   What do you think the girl could have won her medals for?

2   Why did she keep on telling people how clever she was?

3   Why did she have no friends to walk home with?

4   What was the danger in walking home from her school?

5   Are there any possible dangers in walking home from your school?

6   What did she think as she walked through the woods alone?

7   How did the wolf know where she was hiding?

8   Do we know what happened to the girl?

9   Do you think the story really happened? Could it have happened?

10   What do you think the moral of this story is?

Thinking about modesty and pride

Key question: What do pride and modesty mean?

1   What is pride? What does 'proud as a peacock' mean? What is a 'pride of lions'?

2   What can you be proud of – one's achievements, one's school, one's country?

3   What are you proud of doing?

4 Can one be proud of something which is not true or good? Why? Give an example.

5 Can a person be too proud? What is boasting, arrogance, conceit, and being a snob?

6 What do people boast about? Give an example. Do you ever boast? Why?

7 Some people are modest. What is modesty? Give an example.

8 There is a saying 'Pride comes before a fall'. What does this mean?

9 Some people think they are always right. Can they be?

10 Do we all have something to take pride in?

Further activities

* Draw the story in cartoon form (or one scene from the story).

* Design a medal or certificate of success that someone might win, and say what it is for.

* Discuss what you could include in a school report or record of achievement.

* Act out a story about what happens to a very boastful person.

* Write a rap or poem about what you are proud of.

Thought for the day

'Pride goeth before destruction, and an haughty spirit before a fall.'

(The Bible, Proverbs 16:18)

20 PATIENCE

Orpheus in the Underworld

Orpheus was famed throughout ancient Greece as a poet and musician. He was the son of a king and he played a lyre (a stringed instrument like a guitar) given to him by the god Apollo. When Orpheus sang, people stopped and smiled in wonder at his beautiful voice. Wild animals became tame, and they said even the trees and stones would move to follow the sound.

Orpheus had a young wife called Eurydice whom he loved dearly. For a long while the two were as happy as any two people can be. But one day as Eurydice was walking in the fields she met Aristaeus, a hunter, who said he loved her. At first she thought he was joking but when she saw the madness in his eyes she fled. As she ran she trod on a snake which sank its fangs into her ankle. Eurydice fell and a cold numbness spread through her body. When they found her she was dead.

For three days Orpheus stayed in his house, refusing both food and water. On the fourth day he took his lyre and left his house, determined to try to find Hades, the home of the dead. He climbed mountains and crossed deserts. Neither hunger nor thirst, burning sun nor freezing snow could stop him. He was told that Hades, the Underworld, lay across the sea to the West. He sailed across the grey ocean and came at last to the gates of the Underworld – guarded by Cerberus, a huge three-headed dog.

Orpheus lifted his lyre and began to play. The dog relaxed and grew sleepy. Its eyes closed. Orpheus stepped carefully past and entered the dark cave to the Underworld. Down and down he went until he came to a swift flowing river. There was a ferry waiting to carry dead souls to Hades. At first the ferryman refused to take Orpheus – for he was clearly not dead. But after Orpheus sang to him, he agreed.

At last Orpheus reached the place where dead souls go, where Hades, King of the Underworld, ruled with his servants the Furies. 'I have come for my wife Eurydice,' said Orpheus. 'Death took her from me. I beg you to let me take her back … for I love her.'

'What is love?' growled Hades. 'How can love mean anything to death?'

Orpheus took out his lyre and sang about love. The King and his Furies listened to the music entranced.

'Very well,' said Hades. 'You may take Eurydice back to the land of the living, on one condition. Play your lyre and she will follow you. But beware! You must not look round to see her until you are out in the sun, or Eurydice will be lost forever.'

Orpheus thanked the king and, playing his lyre, made his way back. As he played he listened. Was Eurydice behind him? 'Do not look behind … be patient,' he said to himself. He reached the river where the ferry was waiting. Was Eurydice with him too? He must not look. He continued to play his lyre, staring straight ahead, as the ferry took him back towards the gates of Hades. 'I must be patient …'

As he was climbing the path towards the gate of Hades he saw the huge dog Cerberus, still asleep. Was Eurydice there? 'I must … look.' As he reached the gate he glanced back, and saw that Eurydice was just a few feet from him. She opened her mouth, but in a rustle of wind she sank back into Hades. The gates of the Underworld closed. Orpheus sank to his knees. She was gone forever.

(Greek myth)

Thinking about the story

Key question: What does the story mean?

1 When did this story take place?

2 Who was Orpheus?

3 What happened when Orpheus sang?

4 Who was Eurydice? Why did Eurydice die?

5 Why did Orpheus want to go to Hades? What was Hades?

6 Is Hades a real place?

7 How did Orpheus reach Hades?

8 What questions did Hades ask Orpheus? How might Orpheus have replied?

9 What did Orpheus say to himself as he left Hades? Why did he look behind?

10 What do you think the moral of this story is?

Thinking about patience

Key question: What is patience?

1   People say 'Patience is a virtue'. What is a virtue?

2   What things in your life do you have to be patient about?

3   Do you find it easy or hard to be patient? Why?

4   Are you patient with other people? Who are you patient with?

5   Why do you sometimes need to be patient with other people?

6   Are people patient with you? Give an example.

7   Are people ever impatient with you. Why? Give an example.

8   Are you patient (or impatient) with yourself? When or why?

9   What kinds of work take the most patience to do well?

10 Can you think of a time when your patience was rewarded?

Further activities

• Create a cartoon version of the story.

• Write a short story about patience being rewarded.

• Find out who Job was. What does 'the patience of Job' mean?

• Make a list of things you are patient and impatient about. Share and discuss.

• Create a 'Patience' poster with each person completing the sentence: 'Patience is …'

Thought for the day

> 'Our patience will achieve more than our force.'
> *(Edmund Burke, 1729-1797)*

21 PEACE

Tulsi the Peacemaker

Long ago in India there lived a very fat Maharajah. He was the richest and most powerful king in the whole of India. He ate off gold plates, dressed in the finest silks, and his palace was crowned with ivory towers. Peacocks roamed the palace gardens. His vast army included spearmen and bowmen, chariots and elephants. More than all these things he loved his daughter, the beautiful princess Tulsi.

One day the Maharajah was inspecting his army, riding high in his howdah past rows of bright uniforms and sharp pointed swords. As he rode past the lines of soldiers he thought to himself, 'Why have a large army and never go to war?'

On the following day he ordered his chief minister to send a letter to the neighbouring king. The message read: 'Send me fifty blue pigs or else!' As the messenger hurried off, the Maharajah tapped his tummy and smiled.

Some time later the messenger returned with a note from the neighbouring king. The Maharajah blinked when he read the message: 'We have got no blue pigs for you, and if I had …' So the king was refusing to give the great Maharajah those fifty blue pigs!

'This means war!' shouted the Maharajah.

His great army marched forth with flying banners, the chariot wheels rolled and the earth trembled with the trampling of elephants. The war was as cruel as all wars are. Death and injury made the land wretched. Corpses were left rotting in the fields and houses were burnt. Mothers cried for their dead sons, and waited for fathers who would never return. The war dragged on. What could be done to end it? Only one person knew, and that was the Maharajah's daughter, the beautiful Princess Tulsi. She was determined that the fighting must stop.

'But what can you do?' said her friend. 'How can one person stop two great armies?'

'You are only a girl,' said another. 'No one will listen to you.'

'You are too young to do anything,' said a third.

But all this made Tulsi more determined than ever. She swept past the guards and burst through the great doors of the council chamber.

'I want to see the Maharajah,' she said. 'I want to see the Maharajah.'

The Maharajah stared in surprise. 'Go … go to your room, daughter!' he bellowed. 'War is a business for men, not girls.'

'My dear father,' said Tulsi. 'I do not want to speak of war, I want to talk of peace.'

The Maharajah could hardly believe his ears. No one had ever spoken to him like this before – let alone a mere girl. But before he could speak, Tulsi was saying, 'Why don't you go and talk with your enemy? Ask the king that you are fighting what he meant by his letter. It wouldn't hurt just to talk, would it?'

The old Maharajah could not think of an answer. So it was not long before the Maharajah rode forth to meet his great enemy, the neighbouring king. And Tulsi went too.

When they met, the other king spoke first.

'What did you mean, Maharajah, by your message – "Send fifty blue pigs or else"?'

'Fifty blue pigs,' explained the Maharajah, 'or else white pigs or black pigs, or any other colour that you might have. I would have paid you a good price. But what did you mean by, "We've got no blue pigs for you, and if we had …" ?'

'Oh,' replied the king. 'If you had carried on reading you would have seen. My message was, "We have got no blue pigs for you and if we had I would be most pleased to send them to you."'

At once the kings realised their misunderstanding. The war was stopped, the soldiers came home, and the country returned to peace and plenty. The Maharajah grew in riches, but of all his treasures the one he loved best was his daughter, Tulsi the peacemaker.

(Indian legend)

Thinking about the story

Key question: What does the story mean?

1   Who was the Maharajah?

2   Why do you think he loved Tulsi most of all?

3   Why did he have such a large army?

4   What message did he send to the neighbouring king?

5   What reply did he get?

6   What was the war like?

7   Why was Tulsi determined to stop the war?

8   What plan did Tulsi have to try to stop the war?

9   What causes war? What caused this war?

10 Have you ever tried to make peace between people? When? Why?

Thinking about peace

Key question: What is peace?

1   What is peace? How does it differ from war?

2   Which is better, peace or war? Why?

3   What parts of the world today are without peace? Give an example, and explain why.

4   Can there be lasting peace betwen people? What causes strife between people?

5   How do you help people to end quarrels, disputes and arguments?

6   Are people always at peace within themselves? Why, or why not?

7   What is 'peace of mind'? Do you have it? When is it upset? Give an example, say why.

8   What gives you feelings of peace?

9   What is a 'peace offering'? Have you ever made a peace offering? Give an example.

10   Winston Churchill once said: 'Jaw, jaw is better than war, war.'
What did he mean? Do you agree? Why?

Further activities

- Find newspaper pictures or stories of war and peace. Describe, compare and contrast.

- The symbol of peace is a dove. Design your own symbol, badge or poster for peace.

- Visit a local war memorial or interview an old soldier, sailor or airman about their experience of war.

- Find and/or create examples of music that symbolise peace and strife in sound.

- Research the work of the UN in peace-keeping operations in the world today.

Thought for the day

> 'Blessed are the peacemakers: for they shall be called the children of God.'
>
> *(The Bible, Matthew 5:8)*

22 RESPECT FOR THE ENVIRONMENT

Dead as a Dodo

There was once a large, strange bird called a dodo. But today there are no more dodos and there will never be any more dodos. The last dodo died more than 300 years ago. They are extinct – and this is how it happened.

Many thousand years ago big birds with strong wings flew across the Indian Ocean and landed on the island of Mauritius. There they found many plants, berries and seeds to eat, and no other animals harmed them. They were safe and never went hungry. Life was easy for these birds, and as centuries passed they began to change. They ate a lot and grew fat. No one chased them so they did not have to fly. They never used their wings and eventually became too weak to lift them. They became birds who could no longer fly.

A fully-grown bird weighed over 20 kilograms. They made their nests on the ground, and their eggs were the size of grapefruit. They fed on roots that they dug up with their sharp, hooked beaks. They led peaceful and contented lives, until one day their island was discovered by an altogether different kind of animal – human beings.

Sailors from Portugal discovered the island of Mauritius in 1507. The sailors were hungry and began to look for food. Other birds on the island could fly away, but this bird could not. It was helpless in the face of danger. The sailors caught and killed as many dodos as they could find, and ate the dodo's eggs. They called the bird *doudo*, the Portuguese word for silly. Although the bird was given other names over the years, dodo is the name that stuck.

Later, Dutch, French and English ships stopped there too, and their sailors also hunted the dodo for food. In 1644 the dodos faced a further danger when settlers from Holland came to live on the island, and brought with them cats, dogs, pigs and goats. Some of these animals chased and killed the dodos. Then another kind of animal was brought to the island which posed an even greater danger to the survival of the dodos. Monkeys were introduced and multiplied quickly. Whenever they found a dodo's egg they would eat it. Each year fewer and fewer chicks were hatched, and the numbers of dodos dwindled. The last of these slow, fat birds was seen on Mauritius in 1681.

All that you can see today of the dodo is a skeleton in the museum. You may have heard the expression 'dead as a dodo', which is used to describe something which is gone forever.

Since then many other animals, such as the great auk, have gone forever. Many species are in danger of becoming extinct right now. Unless we protect plants and wildlife from being carelessly destroyed they might one day become extinct – as dead as the dodo.

(Historical account)

> The Dodo used to walk around,
>   And take the sun and air.
> The sun yet warms his native ground -
>   The Dodo is not there!
>
> The voice which used to squawk and squeak
>   Is now forever dumb -
> Yet may you see his bones and beak
>   All in the Mu-se-um.

Hilaire Belloc

Thinking about the story

Key question: What does the account mean?

1   What did a dodo look like? How do you think we know what a dodo looked like?

2   What we know about the history and habits of the dodo?

3   Why did the dodo not fly?

4   Who first discovered the dodo?

5   What did they call the dodo? Why? What other names might it have had?

6   What caused the dodo to become extinct?

7   Could you see a dodo today? If so, where?

8   What does 'as dead as a dodo' mean?

9   What other animals have become extinct? What caused them to become extinct?

10   Do you think all plants and animals could become 'as dead as the dodo'? Why?

Thinking about respect for the environment

Key question: What is respect for the environment?

1   Does it matter if a species of animal such as the dodo becomes extinct? Why?

2   How might the dodo have been preserved from extinction?

3   How can we help to preserve wild birds and animals?

4   Is it right to hunt wild animals? Why or why not?

5   Is it right for humans to eat animals?

6   What is the environment? What are the threats to the environment (sources of pollution)?

7   What does conservation mean?

8   Why should we bother to care for the environment?

9   What is the Country Code? What do you think the Country Code should say about looking after the environment?

10   Should you help conserve the resources of the world? Why? How?

Further activities

*   Make a study of one or more of the world's endangered species.

*   Discuss ways of caring for, conserving and improving a local natural environment.

*   Survey local litter and refuse recycling amenities. Design anti-pollution posters.

*   Research and discuss a current environmental problem or issue in the news.

*   Write a poem or story about the last dodo.

Thought for the day

'The environment is everything that isn't me.'
(Albert Einstein, 1879-1955)

23 RESPECT FOR OTHERS

The Loathly Lady

One day when King Arthur was out hunting he became lost in a wood. Eventually he came to a castle. When he entered he found himself caught in the power of an evil wizard. His strength left him and he fell helpless to the ground. The wizard drew his sword. 'Have pity on me!' cried Arthur.

'Killing you would be too easy,' said the wizard, his voice as cold as death. 'I will spare your life on one condition. Within a year you must return with the right answer to this question: "What do women want most?" If you cannot solve this riddle you will die.'

Arthur set forth on his quest. He asked many people and found many answers, but he knew in his heart that none of them seemed right. When the year was almost up Arthur, without hope, began his journey back to the castle in the wood. On his way he came across a lady sitting by a stream, reading a book. She wore beautiful clothes but when she turned Arthur had a shock. The lady was the ugliest and most loathsome looking person he had ever seen. Her skin was grey and wrinkled, her yellow teeth stuck out like boar's tusks, her eyes were bloodshot red, her hair was like rusty wire and she had three hairy chins. But to his surprise the lady said: 'I know the question you wish to ask, and I know the answer. I will give it to you on one condition.'

'And what is that?' asked Arthur.

'Give me Sir Gawain, the best and bravest of your knights, in marriage to be my husband, and I will give you the answer that will save your life.'

With a heavy heart Arthur told Gawain what the ugly hag had said, and Gawain replied that he would gladly marry the loathly lady to save the king's life. When the marriage between Gawain and the loathly lady was agreed, she then told Arthur the answer to the riddle that had perplexed him for nearly a year. 'Tell me, what is it that women most want?' asked Arthur. She answered: 'What women most want is to be in charge.'

Arthur hurried back to the wizard's castle. The answer he gave proved correct and Arthur's life was saved. There was great rejoicing when the news reached Arthur's court, but they all wondered what Gawain would do now. He did indeed honour his promise and married the old hag.

On the wedding night the loathly lady asked Gawain to give her a kiss. Gawain looked at her boar's tusk teeth, her grey, wrinkled skin and her three hairy chins. Gawain closed his eyes tight and despite his innermost feelings he gallantly kissed her. At once he found himself in the arms of a beautiful woman. His kiss seemed to have broken the spell she was under. But she said there was still one riddle he must answer: 'Would he have her looking fair by night and foul by day, or foul by night and fair by day?'

Gawain knew that there was only one answer he should give. He said: 'Do as you wish, my lady.' At once the spell was broken. By respecting what she wanted Gawain had completely broken the spell. The loathly lady was now fully transformed back into her human shape, becoming fair both night and day. They could now live together in true happiness.

> *(Adapted from 'The Wedding of Sir Gawain and Lady Ragnell',*
> *a 15th century anonymous poem.)*

Thinking about the story

Key question: What does the story mean?

1 Who do you think King Arthur was?

2 How did Arthur find himself in the power of an evil wizard?

3 What riddle did Arthur have to solve?

4 Why was he set this riddle?

5 What answers do you think people gave him to the riddle?

6 Who was the loathly lady? What do you think the word 'loathly' means?

7 What answer to the riddle did the loathly lady give? What did it (or does it) mean?

8 Why did Gawain marry the loathly lady? What do you think he (and she) felt about this?

9 What happened on the wedding night? Why did it happen?

10 Why does the story say they could now live in true happiness?

Thinking about respect for others

Key question: What does respect for others mean?

1 How did the characters in the story show respect for each other?

2 What does 'showing respect' for someone mean?

3 Who (or what) do you respect? How do you show that respect?

4 Who respects you? How do they show they respect you?

5 Is showing respect what you think about, or what you do, for someone?

6 Can you earn someone's respect? How?

7 Can you respect someone you don't like?

8 Is it good to show respect? When? Why?

9 Is it ever right not to show respect to people? Why? Can you give an example?

10 What do you think the moral of this story might be?

Further activities

- Write about 'My hero/heroine is...' Describe who they are. Say why you respect them.

- Discuss reasons why or why not you should respect old people.

- Find out about human rights. Create your own charter of human rights. (See Appendix 2)

- Discuss ways of showing respect to a visitor to your school or home.

- List the ten things you most respect in your life. Share and explain your list.

Thought for the day

'People won't respect you unless you respect them.'

(old saying)

24 RESPECT FOR THE LAW

Note: Teachers may make an OHP.

Thinking about the photograph

Key question: What does the photograph mean?

1   What kind of picture is this?

2   Where is it set?

3   Who is in the picture?

4   Why might the men be running?

5   Where might the men have come from? What might have happened?

6   Where might they be running to?

7   Both men are policemen. Does this surprise you? Why?

8   What might explain this?

9   What would be a suitable title or caption for this picture?

10   This is a police recruitment picture. Why do you think they chose this picture for an advert to recruit more police officers?

Thinking about respect for the law

Key question: What is the law?

1   What is a law?

2   Where do laws come from? Who makes laws?

3   How is the law decided in a democracy? Can laws be changed? How?

4   Who has to obey the law?

5   What happens to people who break the law?

6   Are some laws more important than others?

7   What laws are most important?

8   What is a court of law? How does it work? Why does it work that way?

9   What is the role of the police?

10   Should all laws be obeyed? Can a law be a wrong law?

Further activities

- Act out a trial in a court of law, with the accused, defence and prosecution lawyers, judge and jury.

- Hold a debate about a currently controversial issue with everyone in the jury giving a verdict.

- Discuss and create 10 'laws' to keep the peace in your classroom, home or community.

- Design a recruitment poster for the police.

- Interview a local policeman, magistrate or someone from the legal profession about the working of the law.

Thought for the day

'Love is the fulfilling of the law.'

(The Bible, Romans 15:10)

25 RESPONSIBILITY

Val's Problem Page

Dear Val,

My Mum's really winding me up. On the one hand she's always asking me to help out, do things in the house, look after my little brothers for her so she can go out and do the shopping and things. She really dumps on me sometimes and expects me to give up my own life just to be at home and be part of 'the family'. But when I go out with my friends and have a good time she gets all protective and says that I'm not old enough to be sensible and responsible.

She makes a fuss about me staying over at parties and rings me on my mobile if I'm even one minute late home. Now I want to go with a crowd of people to camp at a festival and she won't let me. But the next weekend she wants to go away with her boyfriend and I'm supposed to stay home and look after the kids and everything. How can I be old enough to look after them when she says I'm not old enough to look after myself?

Danielle, Walsall.

Dear Danielle,

You don't say how old you are and that makes a big difference in this situation. Age doesn't necessarily go hand in hand with being responsible of course, but if you're very young you simply haven't had to face as many problems and make as many decisions as someone older. Being in charge of young children like your brothers is a lot to ask of a teenager. I think you need to talk to your Mum about whether there isn't someone who can move in with you all for the weekend while she's away, just to give you some support.

It sounds as if you are a great help at home. I'm sure your Mum appreciates how much you do for her. Probably she can't imagine how to cope without you.

I expect she's finding it hard to accept that you are beginning to move away from her to find your own life. It is hard for parents to let go and give their children their independence. She wants to look after you, or at least know that you're OK, and she doesn't want to admit that family life is changing.

Pop festivals are rather overwhelming and scary, as well as exciting. Perhaps you could just go for the day this time, and then maybe stay next year when you know a bit more about the set-up? If you make a sensible suggestion like this, perhaps that will convince her that you are more grown-up and responsible than she thinks.

Val

(from the problem page of a magazine)

Thinking about the problem

Key question: What is the problem?

1   What is Danielle's problem? How does she think her Mum is winding her up?

2   What does it mean for someone to be 'winding you up'? What 'winds you up'?

3   What does Danielle want to do? Why?

4   What do you think Danielle means by having to 'stay at home and look after the kids and everything'?

5   How old do you think Danielle might be? Does it matter how old Danielle is?

6   Why do you think her mother makes a fuss when Danielle is late home from a party? Do you think she is right to?

7   What is Val's answer to Danielle? What does she say Danielle should do? Why?

8   What does Val think about Danielle's mother?

9   Do you think Val has given Danielle a good answer? Why? What answer would you give?

10   Do you think writing to a magazine for advice is a good idea? Why? Who else could Danielle talk to about her problems?

Thinking about responsibility

Key question: What does responsibility mean?

1   What does it mean to be responsible for someone? Give an example.

2   Do you have to take responsibility for looking after anyone?

3   Are you responsible for looking after yourself? Who is responsible for looking after you? Why?

4   How old do you think children should be before they are considered to be adults?

5   How old do you think children should be before they are left at home by themselves?

6   When should children be asked to look after their younger brothers or sisters?

7   How late should children be allowed to say out at night? Why?

8   What does it mean to be 'grown up and responsible'? Are all grown-ups responsible?

9   What is the opposite of responsible? Give an example of being irresponsible.

10   Is it good to have responsibilities? Why/why not?

Further activities

• Act out an argument between Danielle and her mother.

• Imagine you are Val. Discuss and write the reply *you* would give to Danielle.

• Collect examples of problem page letters from newspapers and magazines to discuss.

• Ask each person or pair in the group to write a letter about a pretend problem in their lives. Share these around. Each reads and responds to the problem letter they receive.

• Write a recipe for a perfect mother, father, or friend.

Thought for the day

'Am I my brother's keeper?'

(The Bible, Genesis 4:9)

26 SELF CONTROL

The Talking Turtle

There was once a fellow called Cary. The trouble with Cary was that he could not keep anything to himself. He was a great chatterbox. Whenever anybody had done something which was not right, Cary would run and tell everyone about it. He never told lies, he just told the truth and that's what made it so bad. Everyone believed what Cary said, and there was no way you could pretend he was making it up.

When he was young he would always tell the teacher if he saw somebody pinch someone else, or if they said a rude word. He would always tell who it was that made a rude noise. He was always talking when he should have been listening. When he was alone he would even talk to himself. The sure way to spread a story about someone was to tell it to Cary.

As Cary grew older he got no better. No secrets were safe when he was around. No boy could have a girlfriend, and no girl could have a boyfriend, without Cary spreading the word. Nothing seemed to stop Cary's gossiping. Nothing, that is, until the time he found a turtle in the road. The turtle was bigger than the common kind, so Cary stopped to look at it. The old turtle winked its eyes and said, 'Cary, you talk too much!'

Cary jumped four feet in the air, and then just stood there with his mouth hanging open. He looked all round, but there was nobody in sight. 'My ears must be back to front,' he said to himself. 'Everyone knows that turtles are dumb.'

The old turtle winked its red eyes again. 'Cary, you talk too much,' said the turtle. With that Cary spun round like a top and headed back for home.

When Cary told his friends about the turtle they just laughed in his face. 'You come with me,' he said, 'and I'll show you!'

So the whole crowd went along, but when they got there the turtle never said a word. It looked just like any other turtle, only bigger than the usual sort. Cary tried talking to it, but the turtle's mouth never moved. The crowd of people were fed up with having to go all that way for nothing. They jeered at Cary for telling tall stories, and left him standing there. Cary looked sadly at the turtle, and the old turtle winked its red eyes and said, 'Didn't I tell you? You talk too much.'

Some people said the whole thing was a joke, because it isn't possible for turtles to talk. Perhaps someone was hiding in the bushes and throwing his voice so it just sounded as if the turtle was talking. Everyone knows that ventriloquists can make dummies talk well enough to fool almost anybody. But none of Cary's friends were good enough for that, in fact no one in town could throw his voice like that.

Whether it was a joke or not, the turtle stopped old Cary's chatter. Whenever he came up with one of his stories, his friends would just laugh and say, 'Go and tell the turtle, Cary, go and tell the turtle.'

(*American folktale*)

Thinking about the story

Key question: What does the story mean?

1   What was the trouble with Cary?

2   What did he tell his teacher? Why did he say that?

3   What did he do when he was alone? Why did he do this?

4   Why could he not keep a secret?

5   What did the turtle say to Cary? Why did the turtle say this?

6   What did Cary think of the turtle?

7   What did his friends think?

8   What happened when they all went to see the turtle?

9   Did the turtle stop Cary talking so much?

10   Do you think Cary's habits would have changed after this? Why?

Thinking about self control

Key question: What is self control?

1   When is it good to talk?

2   Is it possible to talk too much?

3   When is it good not to say anything, and better to keep quiet?

4   Has anyone ever said anything to you that they did not mean to say?

5   Have you ever said anything that you regretted saying? Explain the circumstances.

6   Can you control everything you say?

7   There is a saying: 'Sticks and stones can break my bones but words can never harm me'. What does it mean? Is it true?

8   Can you control what you think? Can you always control what you do?

9   Is it better to be controlled by others or to control yourself?

10   What is self control? Is it a good thing? Why?

Further activities

- Tape record yourself. Talk in different voices and accents. Try to disguise your voice.

- Play 'Just a minute'. Each player has to talk for one minute on a chosen subject.

- Make up a story about an animal that suddenly starts talking to someone.

- Make a list of things you can control, and things you cannot control.

- Each write a letter to an imaginary 'agony aunt' explaining a bad habit you have, then write a reply to one of the letters offering advice on how to overcome the problem.

Thought for the day

'They never taste who always drink:
They always talk who never think.'

(Matthew Prior, 1664-1721)

27 SHARING

Sharing the Fish

In a certain village in India there once lived a holy man, a Brahman, who had a wife. One day the Brahman's wife decided she would like some fish for supper. So she asked her husband to go to market to buy her some fresh fish.

The Brahman returned with three fine fresh fish, and soon they were cooking on the fire. They smelt good! The Brahman sat ready for his dinner. 'I shall eat two of these fish,' he said.

'Oh no you won't,' said his wife, 'I'm having two.'

'What!' said the Brahman. 'I bought them, so I deserve the biggest share.'

'I have to cook them,' said the wife.

'I am lord and master of this house!' shouted the Brahman.

'I am your wife! You promised to love and cherish me!'

What a row they had! The argument went on all evening, their voices getting louder and louder, and all the time they were feeling hungrier and hungrier. At last the Brahman said 'Wait! I know how to settle this. Let us go to bed, and whoever speaks first shall have only one fish.'

'Very well,' said the wife. So they lay side by side in bed not daring to speak. Darkness came. The fish lay cold on the table and not a word was spoken. The next morning they were still there, in the silent house.

Usually they were a noisy pair and when no sound could be heard their neighbours began to worry. They knocked on the door and called out, but there was no reply. At last they decided to break in and see if something was wrong. When they forced the door open they saw a strange sight. The Brahman and his wife lay there with their eyes open, not saying a word.

One of the neighbours shook and slapped them but there was no reaction. 'Oh dear,' he said. 'They must be dead.'

At once they began to prepare the funeral. Sadly they carried the Brahman and his wife to the river bank where, according to Hindu custom, the bodies of the dead were burnt. With many tears they placed the Brahman and his wife on a bed of logs. Someone took a torch and lit the funeral pyre.

As the flame licked the Brahman's foot he gave a great yell. 'Aaaah! I will have only one fish!'

'Then I shall have two!' shouted his wife in triumph.

The neighbours fell back in amazement, then ran for their lives as they saw what looked like two hungry ghosts coming towards them. The Brahman and his wife chased after them, back to their house for their breakfast of three cold fish.

(Indian folktale)

Thinking about the story

Key question: What does the story mean?

1   Where does this story take place?

2   The Brahman is a holy man. What is a 'holy man'?

3   Why did the man and wife have a row?

4   What plan did they have to settle the argument? Was it a good plan?

5   What did the neighbours do? What did they think?

6   What was the Hindu custom with dead bodies?

7   What happened at the funeral?

8   Who won the argument?

9   What could have prevented the argument in the first place?

10   Have you ever argued with someone about sharing things? What happened?

Thinking about sharing

Key question: What is sharing?

1   What does it mean to share something?

2   What should you share? Should shares be equal? Why or why not?

3   Are there some things you would never share?

4   Should you ever share a secret?

5   Who shares things with you? Why do they do that?

6   What do you have to share with others?

7   What do you want others to share with you?

8   Should a family share the work of running a home? Why?

9   Do some people find it very difficult to share? Why is that?

10   What would you say to someone who refused to share anything with anyone else?

Further activities

- Create a newsboard, newsletter or email to share news and views with others.

- Research the work of an international aid organisation. Discuss how rich countries might best share their wealth with poor countries.

- Discuss problems in sharing out work in a home, classroom or community.

- Discuss religious significance of sharing meals eg Christain communion. Create a meal to share with others.

- Make up some rules for a happy home.

Thought for the day

'Trouble is part of your life, and if you don't share it, you don't give the person who loves you a chance to love you enough.'

(Dinah Shore)

28 THOUGHTFULNESS

The Ten Pound Note

Mrs Brown was on her way to London. It was her birthday and she had a brand new £10 note which her husband and children had given her as a present. As she climbed aboard the London train she was wondering what she would buy with her money. There was one other person in her carriage, a shabby-looking old lady clutching a handbag, who was fast asleep.

Mrs Brown put her own bag down beside her and soon she dozed off too, dreaming of a new hat. The train rattled and jolted. After a while Mrs Brown woke up. She had a strange feeling that something was wrong. She glanced at her watch and realised the train would soon be arriving at the station. She opened her handbag and looked for her ticket. When she looked inside her bag she got a surprise. The ticket was there but she could not see her £10 note. Had she lost it? Hurriedly she searched her bag and her pockets. There was no sign of the money. Where could it have gone?

Mrs Brown did not know what to do. She looked across at the scruffy old woman, who still seemed to be fast asleep. Would she have taken it? When Mrs Brown was asleep the old lady could have leaned across and taken the money. How else could it have gone?

Mrs Brown thought she would find out whether her suspicion was correct. She leaned across and peered into the old lady's handbag. In the corner of the bag was a tatty purse. Mrs. Brown slowly removed the purse, and opened it. To her surprise she saw a new £10 note.

Mrs Brown was speechless with anger. 'Thief!' she thought. She felt like hitting the old woman. Should she wake the old lady and accuse her of stealing? Should she call a guard on the train, or wait till she found a policeman at the station? No, she had a better idea. Mrs Brown carefully took the £10 note from the old lady's bag and tucked it into her own handbag. Perhaps she would forgive the old lady; after all she was poor and Mrs Brown had got her money back. So she did not say a word about it. The train pulled into the station. Mrs Brown took one last look at the sleeping old lady, got off and went to the shops.

After a great day's shopping Mrs Brown went home with a new hat in her bag. As soon as she got in she said to her husband: 'You'll never guess what happened to me today.'

'I know,' said her husband, 'you forgot your £10 note. I found it on the table after you'd gone. Here it is.' He took the note from his pocket and gave it to her.

Mrs Brown could not say a word. At once she realised the old lady had not stolen her £10 note after all. Mrs Brown was heartbroken. 'How did it happen?' she thought. 'How did I make such a terrible mistake?'

(A modern legend)

Thinking about the story

Key question: What does the story mean?

1   Why was Mrs Brown on her way to London?

2   Who else was in her carriage?

3   Why did Mrs Brown have a feeling when she woke up that something was wrong?

4   Why could she not find the £10 note in her handbag? Why did she feel angry?

5   Why did she think the old lady had stolen it?

6   What did Mrs Brown decide to do? Was this a good idea? Why?

7   Why did she not say anything to the old lady? What would you have done?

8   What 'terrible mistake' did Mrs Brown realise she had made when she got home?

9   Why did she think the mistake was 'terrible'? Do you agree it was terrible? Why?

10   What lesson do you think Mrs Brown learnt from what happened?

Thinking about being thoughtful

Key question: What is thoughtfulness?

1   Has anyone thought you had done something wrong when you hadn't? How did you feel?

2   Have you ever thought someone had done something wrong
    when they hadn't? How did you or they feel?

3   Have you ever seen someone else being accused wrongly? What
    do you think they felt?

4   Do people ever do or say things without thinking? Why? Do you
    ever do things without thinking? When? Why?

5   Is it easy or hard to think of things from another person's point
    of view? Why?

6   Is it ever possible to know what other people are thinking?

7   Can stopping to think help stop mistakes or accidents
    happening? Give an example.

8   What does 'jumping to conclusions' mean?

9   What does 'thoughtfulfulness' mean?

10 Are you a thoughtful person? What helps you to think? What
    stops you thinking?

Further activities

- Write, act or present the story from the old woman's or
  husband's point of view.

- Discuss what you could, should and would do if you found a £10
  note.

- Give every child a 'Thinkbook' and time to write their thoughts,
  questions, and feelings.

- Design a poster for a purpose with the slogan: 'Think First'.

- Read the poem 'A poison tree' by William Blake. Write a poem
  about anger.

Thought for the day

'He who never made a mistake never made a discovery.'
(Samuel Smiles, 1812-1904)

29 TOLERATION

The Bully Asleep

This afternoon, when grassy
Scents through the classroom crept,
Bill Craddock laid his head
Down on his desk and slept.

5   The children came round him:
Jimmy, Roger and Jane;
They lifted his head timidly
And let it sink again.

'Look, he's gone sound asleep, Miss,'
10 Said Jimmy Adair;
'He stays up all night, you see;
His mother doesn't care.'

'Stand away from him children.'
Miss Andrews stooped to see.
15 'Yes, he's asleep; go on
With your writing, and let him be.'

'Now's a good chance!' whispered Jimmy;
And he snatched Bill's pen and hid it.
'Kick him under the desk, hard;
20 He won't know who did it.'

'Fill all his pockets with rubbish -
Paper, apple-cores, chalk.'
So they plotted, while Jane
Sat wide-eyed at their talk.

25 Not caring, not hearing,
Bill Craddock he slept on;
Lips parted, eyes closed -
Their cruelty gone.

'Stick him with pins!' muttered Roger.
30 'Ink down his neck!' said Jim.
But Jane, tearful and foolish,
Wanted to comfort him.

John Walsh

Thinking about the story

Key question: What does the poem mean?

1 What was the setting of the poem (when/where did it take place)?

2 Who were the characters named in the poem?

3 Who was 'the bully' that the poem is about? How do we know he was 'the bully'?

4 Why had Bill Craddock fallen asleep? What reasons could explain his falling asleep?

5 What does it mean when the poem says 'His mother doesn't care' (line 12)?

6 What did others suggest doing while he was asleep? Should they be allowed? Why?

7 Why did Miss Andrews say 'go on/with your writing, and let him be' (lines 15/16)?

8 What do the lines 'Lips parted, eyes closed -/Their cruelty gone'(lines 27/8) mean?

9 Why did Jane want to comfort him? Why might Jane be described as 'tearful and foolish' (line 31)?

10 What do you think happened next, after the poem ends?

Thinking about toleration and bullying

Key question: What behaviour by others should, and should not be tolerated?

1 Children are sometimes allowed to do things in school that teachers do not like. Can you think of an example?

2 Should children ever be permitted to fall asleep in the classroom? Why?

3 What things should a teacher never allow (or tolerate) children doing in a classroom?

4 Do you think bullying should be tolerated in school? (If not, what can be done about it?)

5 What kinds of bullying are there? What is a bully? Why do some people bully others?

6   If you found a bully asleep what would you think or do?

7   If someone was being bullied what should they do?

8   Have you ever been bullied? Explain what happened.

9   What things that you do not like should you tolerate (eg friends making fun of you)?

10   What things that other people do should you not tolerate? Why?

Further activities

- Ask small groups to act out situations where bullying occurs. Discuss different possible scenarios and solutions to the problems presented.

- Write a story or poem with 'The bully...' as part of the title.

- Find and share examples of bullying in fiction eg Flashman in *Tom Brown's Schooldays*.

- Brainstorm and list as many kinds of bullying as you can eg 'Bullying is ...'

- Read and discuss 'When Fingal faced a Bully' (*Stories for Thinking* p 30)

Thought for the day

'I disapprove of what you say, but I will defend to the death your right to say it.'

(Voltaire, 1694-1778)

30 WISDOM

Solomon and the Baby

In far-off days, so the Bible tells us, there was a king named Solomon. Everyone loved Solomon, for he was a good and wise king. Whenever they had any troubles the people knew that Solomon would always listen and try to help them. Each morning he would sit on a great throne in his court and wait to see who would come to ask for his help.

One day a great noise was heard as two women came into court arguing at the tops of their voices. 'Silence in court!' said the Captain of the Guard. The women stopped arguing.

'Now tell me,' said Solomon, 'what is wrong ... one at a time, please!'

'Great king,' said one of the women, 'you must decide between this woman and myself. We both live in the same house and a little while ago each of us had a baby. One night this woman's baby died. She was very sad and then she did a terrible thing. At night while I was asleep she crept into my room and stole my baby. She says that it is my baby that died, and the live baby is hers. I cannot prove the baby is mine, but it is.'

Then the other woman spoke. 'The baby is mine. What this woman says about one baby dying is true, but the baby who died was hers. Now she has no baby, and she wants to take mine.'

Solomon looked at the two women and then said, 'Bring the baby here.' In a few minutes the tiny baby was brought in and placed in front of Solomon. 'As you both say the baby is yours I have decided that the baby shall be cut in two, and that each mother shall have half the baby. It is the only fair thing to do, don't you agree?'

Solomon then took out his sword, raised it high above his head, and waited.

'O wise king,' said the first woman, 'whatever you say is right.'

'No, no!' shouted the second woman. 'Please don't kill the baby! Let her have him. I'd rather the baby were hers than killed.'

Solomon smiled, lowered his sword and said to her, 'You are the true mother of the child, for no real mother who loved her baby would want to see him killed.' Solomon handed the baby to the true mother who took the child happily into her arms. Once more Solomon had shown that he was a good and wise king.

(The Bible, 1 Kings 3)

Thinking about the story

Key question: What does the story mean?

1   Who was Solomon?

2   Why did people come to see Solomon?

3   Why were the two women quarrelling?

4   Could both the women be telling the truth?

5   How would you have tried to solve the problem?

6   What did Solomon say he would do to the baby?

7   Why did he say that?

8   Why did one of the woman say 'let her have him'?

9   Do you think Solomon found the true mother?

10   Was Solomon a wise man? Why?

Thinking about wisdom

Key question: What does wisdom mean?

1   What does it mean to be wise?

2   Do you need to know a lot to be wise? What do you need to know to be wise?

3   Is wisdom the same as common sense? What is 'common sense'?

4   A wise decision is a good decision. What is the best way to make a good decision?

5   What sort of person could be called wise?

6   Can anybody be wise, or only someone special? Why?

7   Are you born wise or do you become wise? (If so, how do you become wise?)

8   In the past some wise people were called philosophers. They
     studied philosophy. What is philosophy?

9   Do you have to be old to be wise? What could help you to
     become wise?

10   'The wise old owl sat in an oak
     The more he heard the less he spoke
     The less he spoke the more he heard
     Why can't we be like that wise old bird?'

     Why is the owl thought to be wise?

Further activities

* Find the story of Solomon in the Bible (see 1 Kings 3). Compare
  and discuss different translations of the story.

* Discuss the most important things that a baby needs (food,
  warmth, clothes, love?).

* Find out more about Solomon, the temple of Solomon, Solomon
  and Sheba etc.

* Write the story of Solomon and the baby from the point of view
  of one of the characters.

* Many sayings of the past are remembered as proverbs. Collect
  and discuss favourite proverbs.

Thought for the day

'The price of wisdom is above rubies.'

(The Bible, Psalms 28:18)

Appendices

Appendix 1: Elements of Emotional Intelligence

Self awareness
Observing yourself and recognising your feelings; building a vocabulary for feelings; knowing the relationship between thoughts, feelings and reactions.

Personal decision making
Examining your actions and knowing their consequences; being aware when thoughts or feelings are involved in personal decisions; applying these insights to issues and problems.

Managing feelings
Being aware of what you are feeling; monitoring 'self-talk' to catch negative messages such as internal put-downs; finding ways to handle fears, anxieties, anger and sadness.

Handling stress
Learning the value of exercise, guided imagery, relaxation methods.

Empathy
Understanding the feelings of others and being able to look from their perspective; appreciating that people feel differently about things.

Communication
Talking about feelings effectively; becoming a good listener and asker of questions; being able to communicate your thoughts and feelings with others.

Self-disclosure
Valuing openness and building trust in a relationship; knowing when it's safe to talk about your private feelings.

Insight
Identifying patterns in your own emotional life and reactions and recognising similar patterns in others.

Self acceptance
Seeing yourself in a positive light, recognising your strenghts and weaknesses and being able to laugh at yourself.

Personal responsibility
Taking responsibility; recognising the consequences of your decisions and actions; accepting your own feelings and moods; abiding by commitments.

Confidence
Stating your concerns and feelings without undue anger or passivity.

Cooperation
Being able to co-operate with others; knowing when to lead and follow.

Conflict resolution
Knowing how to resolve conflicts with other children, with parents and other adults; using the win/win model to negotiate a compromise.

Appendix 2: The Convention on the Rights of the Child

The Convention on the Rights of the Child was adopted by the United Nations on 20 November 1989. The following is a summary of its articles:

Article 1: The Convention defines a child as a person under 18.

Article 2: All the rights laid down are to be enjoyed by children regardless of race, colour, sex, language, religion, political or other opinion, national, ethnic or social origin, property, disability, birth or other status.

Article 3: All sections should be in her/his best interests.

Article 4: The State is obliged to translate the rights of the Convention into reality.

Article 5: The State should respect the rights and responsibilities of parents to provide guidance appropriate to the child's capacities.

Every child has:

Article 6: The right to life.

Article 7: The right to a name and a nationality, to know and be cared for by her/his parents.

Article 8: The right to protection of her/his identity by the State.

Article 9: The right to live with her/his parents, and to have contact with both parents if separated from one or both.

Article 10: The right to leave and enter her/his own country, and other countries, for the purposes of maintaining the child-parent relationship.

Article 11: The right to protection by the State if unlawfully taken or kept abroad by a parent.

Article 12: The right to freely express an opinion in all matters affecting her/him and to have that opinion taken into account.

Article 13: The right to express views, and obtain and transmit ideas and information regardless of frontiers.

Article 14: The right to freedom of thought, conscience and religion, subject to appropriate parental guidance.

Article 15: The right to meet together with other children and join and form associations.

Article 16: The right to protection from arbitrary and unlawful interference with privacy, family home and correspondence, and from libel and slander.

Article 17: The right to access of information, and protection from harmful materials.

Article 18: The right to benefit from child-care services provided by the State.

Article 19: The right to protection from maltreatment by parents or others responsible for her/his care.

Article 20: The right to special protection if s/he is temporarily or permanently deprived of her/his family environment.

Article 21: The right, in countries where adoption is allowed, to ensure it is carried out in her/his best interests.

Article 22: The right, if a refugee, to special protection.

Article 23: The right, if disabled, to special care, education and training to help her/him enjoy a full life in conditions which ensure dignity, promote self reliance and a full and active life in society.

Article 24: The right to the highest standard of health and medical care attainable.

Article 25: The right, if placed by the State for purposes of care, protection or treatment, to have all aspects of that placement regularly evaluated.

Article 26: The right to benefit from social security.

Article 27: The right to a standard of living adequate for her/his physical, mental, spiritual, moral and social development.

Article 28: The right to an education, including free primary education. Discipline to be consistent with a child's human dignity.

Article 29: The right to an education which prepares her/him for an active responsible life as an adult in a free society which respects others and the environment.

Article 30: The right, if a member of a minority community or indigenous people, to enjoy her/his own culture, to practise her/his own religion and use her/his own language.

Article 31: The right to rest and leisure, to engage in play and to participate in recreational, cultural and artistic activities.

Article 32: The right to protection from economic exploitation and work that is hazardous, interferes with her/his education, health, physical, mental, spiritual, moral and social development.

Article 33: The right to protection from narcotic drugs and from being involved in their production and distribution.

Article 34: The right to protection from sexual exploitation and abuse.

Article 35: The right to protection from being abducted, sold or trafficked.

Article 36: The right to protection from all other forms of exploitation.

Article 37: The right not to be subjected to torture or degrading treatment. If detained not to be kept with adults, sentenced to death nor imprisoned for life without the possibility of release. The right to legal assistance and contact with family.

Article 38: The right, if below 15 years of age, not to be recruited into armed forces nor to engage in direct hostilities.

Article 39: The right if a victim of armed conflict, torture, neglect or maltreatment or exploitation, to receive appropriate treatment for her/his physical and psychological recovery.

Article 40: The right if accused or guilty of committing an offence, to age-appropriate treatment likely to promote her/his sense of dignity and worth, and her/his reintegration as a constructive member of society.

Article 42: The right to be informed of these principles and provisions by the state in which s/he lives.

Note: Articles 41-54 are concerned with the implementation of these rights.